I am confident that these words will repla[...] what surrender to God truly looks like, with the simplistic truth of what saying yes to God can do for your life. This book is for anyone who craves true surrender to Our Father & complete access to intimacy with Him. Morgan writes with vulnerability about what the ups and downs of this journey look like in an individual's life. I promise that in reading this book you will feel deeply & connect with the truths shared.

Jessica Ellis, Marriage and Family Therapy Associate

"Because God Told Me To" is the book for anyone in the midst of making hard choices. Morgan has shared her experience of God's direction and faithfulness in a relatable and approachable way. Her words are full of both comfort and challenge and you will come away with a sense of confidence in what God is telling you to do! Don't miss out on the wisdom in these pages!

Kelsey Lasher, author

I've had a front row seat watching the author live out the content of this book! Morgan has written an outstanding guide for following the voice of God into the unknown adventure he has for each of us. It's inspiring, funny, and so practical.

Scotty Priest, Lead Pastor, Journey Church Colorado

Because God Told Me To

*a testimony of the power that comes
from complete surrender*

MORGAN COLANDER

Because God Told Me To:

A Testimony of the Power that Comes from Complete Surrender

Print ISBN: 978-1-7378385-0-0

Hardcover ISBN: 978-1-7378385-1-7

eBook ISBN: 978-1-7378385-2-4

Audiobook ISBN: 978-1-7378385-3-1

Cover design and typesetting by Let's Get Booked

www.letsgetbooked.com

To my girl Maliyah, my best friend, my surprise blessing, and dream come true. Thank you for making my world a bigger place, for softening my heart so I can love better, and for being a vessel through which our Father has displayed so much of His goodness and love to me. You inspired this.

I'm so glad you're here.

Introduction

my why

my why

I used to live with my fists tightly closed; now,
I (try my best to) live with my hands wide open in surrender.

Hi, I'm Morgan and I'm a recovering control freak.

I'm a recovering perfectionist.

I'm a recovering judgmentalist (if that even is a word).

I'm simply recovering. I'm being transformed. Renewed. Refined. Freed. Healed. Made whole. Made new.

For the last twelve years my Father has been turning my world upside down. Renewing my heart, transforming my life, and doing ridiculous, outlandish, and overwhelming things. Yet, in hindsight, it all makes perfect sense.

I say this all started twelve years ago because that's the moment my whole world changed. It's the moment He began this deep work in my heart. It's the moment I caught a glimpse into how wonderful His plans are compared to ours, and I experienced the beauty and power that comes from surrender.

Because of my parents' obedience to His plans and their desire to surrender to His will, I received the best gift, ever.

It will forever be one of my favorite phone calls. A baby girl had been born, and she needed a home. Hers was not deemed safe. Without knowing the story that would unfold, our family all agreed she was coming home from the hospital to be with us. We were not a foster family looking to adopt, so I was told time and time again, "Morgan, remember, don't get too attached." Fortunately, that is not how my heart works and with one look at her, my heart was forever tied to hers.

I was thirteen years old, and she was two days old. This is where our story began.

She became my whole world. My days revolved around her – caressing her, rocking her, playing with her, feeding her, loving her.

A year and a half later, a man in a black gown with a wooden mallet named her an official Colander. We had all fallen too much in love to let her go. My prayer of having a sister had been answered.

And so our story continued to unfold. Two Colander sisters doing life together.

It is no ordinary sisterhood though. With a thirteen-year age gap, I get to play the best role. I get to mentor and love, but also take her on sister dates, give her the extra dose of sugar, and tell her all my embarrassing moments from when I was her age.

We laugh until our sides ache, we ride roller coasters until our heads are spinning, and we live life to the fullest.

Our bond has become one I'm unable to describe. It simply takes seeing us together to know we have something special.

All I know is our relationship was one specially crafted by our Father. One He deemed special, significant, and one that will bring Him glory.

Ever since she was placed in my arms, she has brought me joy I did not know existed. Joy that takes the most mundane of days and turns them into my favorite moments. She has provided me with unexplainable peace. Peace that puts my heart to rest because she is proof our Father takes care of us. She is the vessel through which our Father has displayed so much of His goodness and love to me. His joy and peace. His power and majesty.

Through her I see the perfection of His plans. The power He enables us with. The joy He offers us. The gentleness He caresses us with. The love He overwhelms us with. Through her I see Him.

Because of her, I have fallen more in love with my Father than I could ever have imagined.

Because of her and the way she has changed my heart, I find Him in everything and am transformed by it all. The littlest of moments now speak life into my soul and fill my lungs with the air to breathe. Now, in every sunset and sunrise, every rainstorm and sunny day, every word of kindness and embrace of a person, I see Him. I hear Him. I feel Him.

She has softened my heart, so I can love better. She has humbled my heart, so I can see how much I need Him. She has strengthened my heart, so I can fight for His glory. She is the vessel through which He has shown me how much He loves me and will fight for me. She has shown me the radical power that comes when you find rest in the truth that He is holding His children in the palm of His hands, and nothing in this world can change that.

• • •

Twelve years ago, God began this great work in my heart…showing me the way He sees things and teaching me to love people with the kind of grace He offers.

In various ways He began to reveal to me how good His plans are for His children and that if we will choose Him and His will, joy and peace will surely follow.

Surrendering everything to Him will not leave us empty, rather it will fill us until we are overflowing.

The longer life has gone on, the more my heart has begun to burst at the seams reveling in the work He has done in my life and the things He is teaching me. I can't keep quiet any longer.

Hence, this book.

HE BEGAN TO REVEAL TO ME HOW GOOD HIS PLANS
ARE FOR HIS CHILDREN AND THAT IF WE WILL
CHOOSE HIM AND HIS WILL, JOY AND
PEACE WILL SURELY FOLLOW.

In Luke 8:39 after Jesus heals a demon-possessed man He says, *"Return to your home, and declare how much God has done for you."* I believe one of the most powerful ways to learn about the character and truth of our Father is through the stories of others and the ways He has worked in the lives of His children. He calls us to proclaim His name and share the work He has done in our lives so it might bring Him glory. Our miraculous transformation performed through the power of our mighty God was never meant to be a secret. We were never meant to be silent.

While this world often tears down those who boldly proclaim His mighty hand in our lives, we are still called and equipped to share it with others.

So here it is. A bit of my story. The story of the work He is doing in me and through me. A story that has drastically changed my world, but also has the power to change the hearts of those reading it.

> OUR MIRACULOUS TRANSFORMATION
> PERFORMED THROUGH THE POWER OF
> OUR MIGHTY GOD WAS NEVER MEANT TO BE A
> SECRET. WE WERE NEVER MEANT TO BE SILENT.

I pray that through my words, He intercedes. That in reading this piece of my story, He speaks to you and reveals Himself to you in ways neither you nor I could ever have imagined. I pray this book will honor Him and show you more of the truth of who He is.

I pray this book will give you a glimpse into how wonderful and glorious a life lived with Him is. That by reading it you will better understand He truly does love you unconditionally and is worthy of your trust. I pray you will see the only life worth living is one of true and total surrender.

Father, from the beginning You have had Your hand all over this book and more importantly, all over my friends who are reading these words. You created each one of my friends with intention and perfection. Your love for them and plans for them are far greater than anything we could ever comprehend. I'm honored and humbled to know they are choosing to read my words. Father, please speak through these pages. Meet my friends right where they are. Give them a glimpse into how wonderful and glorious a life lived with You is. Amen.

THE ONLY LIFE WORTH LIVING
IS ONE OF
TRUE AND TOTAL SURRENDER.

Chapter one

imperfect, but perfectly made

imperfect, but perfectly made

"Mrs. Seifert, could I please redo this paper or fix it so I can get an A on the assignment?"

My fifth grade teacher just handed back a paper she had recently graded. Assuming I got an A (like always), I flipped the paper over to see I had been given a B.

That was a monumental day in my life...the day I began to realize I was not perfect.

Without hesitation and with a whole lot of panic, I went right up to my teacher and asked to redo the paper or fix it to raise my grade. She said no. I was devastated.

I was not a girl who got B's. I did not do less than perfect work. I was not less than perfect.

Or so I thought...

Up until that point, I didn't know how to handle getting a grade that was less than perfect. I didn't know how to be less than perfect.

My perfectionist side came out early on in my life. There was no hiding it.

11

I grew up going to a charter school, so from kindergarten through eighth grade, I was classmates with about the same sixty kids. Very quickly I earned myself the title of being perfect. I asked a million questions in class, got some of the highest grades, and never got in trouble. I was the salutatorian for my eighth-grade class, and when I found out I had lost to the valedictorian by less than one percent, I was shocked. Second place didn't cut it for me...

Second place wasn't for perfect people. I didn't like the idea of anyone being better than me. I wanted to be recognized as the best. I was so frustrated I had fallen short. Looking back, no one expected perfection from me except me. No one cared I wasn't valedictorian, but I felt I had let everyone down. I had failed to uphold my image of perfection.

High school was the chance to escape my stigma. It was a new school and new classmates...but that didn't last very long.

In a sea of teenagers eager to try new things and teeter with rebellion, I immediately stood out and earned myself the title of being perfect. It was exhausting, but it was who I believed myself to be. I had no choice but to keep striving.

To give you a better idea of how much I stood out, let me draw a picture for you (this is something my older brother likes to remind me of frequently).

For some reason, I had convinced myself that my five-minute passing period wasn't enough time to go to my locker, so instead, I carried every book, binder, and notebook in my giant orange backpack. As soon as the bell rang, I practically sprinted down the hall to my next class. My goal was to get in the front row with about four minutes to spare. Talk about being the cool kid, huh?

In the midst of all my "uncoolness", I was still the girl who got perfect grades. I went to church, went on mission trips, and loved being with my family. I didn't use swear words. I didn't party. Actually, I barely hung out with anyone from high school for the first three years. I kept pretty much to myself, my few friends, and silently judged everyone else.

I stood out like a sore thumb, but still, I couldn't escape this reputation of being perfect.

I was described that way by so many people. The word "perfect" was said to me and said about me, and while I know it is a word meant to flatter, overtime it became paralyzing. It was defining. I was worn out from trying to uphold the image but honestly, I didn't know who I was outside of that neatly packaged and wrapped word.

I went on to graduate college in three years and become a teacher, something I loved and something I was called to. I've traveled all over, always have been involved at my church, have a tendency to be a leader, and I know exactly what I want and what I need to get there.

Simply put, I have always been the girl who did it all and did it well.

Over time, this hasn't just become my reputation, but it is who I have expected myself to be. I am perfect. Or at least I need to try my very hardest to be.

Unfortunately, this world doesn't foster a sense of accepting people where they're at, but rather a need for people to be perfect. It trains us to believe we are never enough and can always strive to be better.

We live in a world that surrounds us with images and ideas of how we can be better. Of how we can inch closer to perfection.

It puts the focus on us. On the "me" side of things, sort of painting us with the "you do you" mentality. It tells us to dig more into the person we want to be...or think we want to be.

YET, WE ARE NOT CALLED TO DO "US";
WE ARE CALLED TO MODEL "HIM."

————

We are called to dig into who our Father is and become someone who reflects Him to the world. He tells us we were made in His image, and we are to be a light to this world.

"You are the light of the world. A town built on a hill cannot be hidden. Neither do people light a lamp and put it under a bowl. Instead they put it on its stand, and it gives light to everyone in the house. In the same way, let your light shine before others, that they may see your good deeds and glorify your Father in heaven."

Matthew 5:14-16

We become the light shining on the darkest of hills by growing in our intimacy with our Father, understanding better who He is, and in turn, choosing to be more like Him.

On the opposite side, the world throws numerous ideas at you to help you become better. Different ways in which you could inch closer to perfection.

You could...

- exercise more.
- switch over to all organic food.
- use safe cleaning products.

- start a blog.
- earn another degree.
- take cuter pictures of your kids.
- grow your own vegetables.
- travel more.
- buy trendier clothes.
- train for a marathon.
- lead a small group.
- get more Instagram followers.

The list is endless.

You could always be more or do more.

The world will always send the same message: You are not enough.

And while we can't control this world and the messages it sends; we can control what we choose to believe. The messages we listen to. The truths we choose to rest in.

And here is the real truth: YOU ARE ENOUGH.

> *"For you created my inmost being; you knit me together in my mother's womb. I praise you because I am fearfully and wonderfully made; your works are wonderful, I know that full well."*

> Psalm 139:13-14

You were perfectly crafted by our Father with such intention and purpose. He says you are enough. He says you are wonderful. He says you are beautiful. He says you are His beloved. He says you are perfectly made.

Perfectly made in His image.

"So God created mankind in his own image, in the image of God he created them; male and female he created them."

Genesis 1:27

This isn't the kind of *perfect* that requires work to get there, but a *perfect* that just is. A perfect that comes from resting in His truth and the sovereignty of His Word. A perfect that comes from reflecting who He is into a world that desperately needs His light.

You are perfect without even trying.

Let that sink in for a minute…

How does that truth make you feel? Do you believe it?

He has called us to be His image bearers. We are called and created to grow in knowing Him so eventually we begin to reflect bits and pieces of our Savior that make Him so perfect.

In understanding what it means to be unconditionally loved by Him, we then reflect His unconditional love to those in our sphere of influence.

As we experience the mercy and grace He so lavishly showers us with, we become people who offer that same thing to those we encounter.

Over time we become aware of the truth that He is a Father who is always present and there when we need Him most, so we become intentional about pouring into the lives of others and supporting people in all seasons.

As we experience who He is, a Father who is everything we need, our hearts are transformed to be more like Him. We become people who aim to bear His image to the people around us, so that in getting

16

glimpses of who He is through us, they begin to crave knowing their Father in a deeply profound and beautiful way.

And even then, we can work our whole lives to become image bearers, and we will still fail tremendously.

Simply put, we are flawed humans who fall short of the glory of God. We are in desperate need of His saving grace and the work He did on the cross. Without Him, we are nothing.

In our state of humanness, we will never be able to fully embody and display who He is. We will fall short of loving people unconditionally. We will pursue judgment over mercy. We will say things and do things we wish we hadn't done.

But that is okay, because our failed attempt to bear His image doesn't change the truth of who He is. He is all-loving, full of mercy and grace, ever present, no matter what. Our imperfect humanness doesn't affect His ability to be a perfect Father.

We are perfectly made to bear His image, and in our shortcomings, He will conquer all.

OUR IMPERFECT HUMANNESS
DOESN'T AFFECT HIS ABILITY
TO BE A PERFECT FATHER.

We don't have to strive to be perfect. We don't have to complete a checklist or compete with the person who seems to do it all. We just need to grow in Him to be more like Him.

• • •

17

While this truth should be enough, sometimes the need to strive, to be everything I think I should be, still battles for my attention. It still dictates so much of my world and how I live my life.

I am a person who wants to do it all. I want to invest in every friendship, lead an active lifestyle, be involved in my church, invest in my musical gifts, spend time outdoors, travel and see the world, volunteer my time to people and places that need it, write, read, and say yes to all the opportunities that come my way. I really want to do it all.

And so I have. I have filled my every waking hour with all these wonderful opportunities and parts of who I am.

To anyone who knows my schedule, it seems impressive. It seems like I have endless energy and stamina. A vigor and a love for life. An inability to tone it down and take a break.

And while all of this is true, I have come to realize my love for life and saying yes to everything is suffocating. There are many days where I feel like I barely have room to breathe.

I'm sure you know exactly what I mean.

I have become quite the master of compartmentalizing my world. There is the category of things I want to worry about, but don't have time to worry about, so I just stuff those things down deep. There is the list of things I have to do every day to feel like a functioning and healthy human being. Then, I have the section of things I need to be planning and thinking about, so I space those out strategically to be sure it all gets done on time. I also have certain people in my life who I feel like I need to check in with every day, people who I'll check in with once a week, and then those I sporadically check in on to be sure they are doing okay. Oh, and don't forget all the hobbies and things

I love that aren't necessary but deserve to be a part of my world. I like to fit those in too. Oh, and then there's all the emotions that go along with life. The ones that sometimes make you feel unstable and like you might be a little off your rocker. Those have to be tended to as well.

Feeling overwhelmed? Yeah, me too.

It's all of that and more. It makes me feel like I am dog paddling with my head barely above water just trying to stay afloat.

Eventually, my strategy of compartmentalizing, making lists, and having a calendar fails me and it all becomes too much. On those days, I am one minimal moment away from a major meltdown. All it takes is dropping my hydro-flask and adding one more dent to it to make me burst into tears.

And it is in these moments that the word "perfect" creeps up on me and tells me I CAN do it all, so I just need to keep pushing.

I begin to hear the lies creep in.

"I mean come on, you are Morgan Colander. You can handle anything."

"People are expecting you to do it."

"You did it before, why can't you do it again?"

"If that person can do it, you should be able to."

And so, I keep pushing. I shove down the emotions, the feelings of being overwhelmed, the fear of the unknown…and I keep going.

I let the pressures of this world – the lies of this world – and the need to prove myself rule my thoughts.

And as soon as I do this – begin to move away from His truth and make space for deceit to plant itself in my heart – the enemy increases his attacks. He creeps in and tells me I must uphold this image of perfection because if I don't, I will let people down. I will let myself down.

The lies swirl around, so I keep going. I keep pushing.

Finally, my Father decides it's enough. He decides I have stood on my pedestal long enough believing I could be everything and do everything. So, He knocks me off.

He brings me to my breaking point where I can no longer be strong on my own. Where I can't hold back the tears anymore. Where the only thing I can do is fall to my knees and rest in His presence.

And always He whispers, "Be still. For you, My child, were not created to be perfect on your own. You were created to be perfect in My image. You were created to be weak, so I could be strong. You were created to fail, so I could succeed. You were created to fall, so I could raise you up. You were created to be My vessel. You were created to need Me. You were created to rest in Me."

He doesn't put me in this place to be malicious. He doesn't do it to flaunt His power.

Instead, He does it to remind me how powerless I am without Him. How weak I am without His strength. How desperately I need Him to be my stronghold.

He is the Father, and He desires for us to be His children.

This means He wants us to realize our need for Him. He wants us to let Him carry the burden and do the heavy lifting. He wants us to rest easy in His arms. He wants us to find stillness in His promise that we are perfectly made to sit and dwell in His sovereignty.

It is in our moments of imperfection that we are reminded of how much we need Him.

In these moments, it is His voice I choose to listen to. His truth I rest in and let calm the unsettled parts of my heart. Here, the peace He offers that surpasses all understanding washes over me. It is in these times I am reminded who holds me and that I am enough, hot mess and all.

The world may swirl in chaos around me, but in these moments, I don't feel the chaos. There is rest instead of exhaustion. Peace instead of worry. I can be still and take a breath.

We get to choose what voice we listen to. You get to choose the voice you believe as truth.

"The mind governed by the flesh is death, but the mind governed by the Spirit is life and peace."

Romans 8:6

• • •

The world won't fall silent until He returns. The lies will continue to swirl. The enemy will continue to find space so he can creep in.

The truth is the world won't just push us to our breaking point, it will push us over the edge. It's up to us not to let it.

The ways of this world and the life it tells us to live will lead to death. There is no other way to say it. The way of this world is death.

It is destructive. It breeds envy, deception, pride, lust, anger, hatred, and discontentment.

And while the world will never be silent, neither will our Father. His truth will never be void. His voice will always have the power to speak louder.

It just requires you to choose to tune into Him and silence everything else.

God only offers us thoughts and opportunities that are in line with His plan. He will only ever lead us in the right direction. He desires to refine, renew, and transform our minds and hearts. Sometimes this means He will break us, but only so He can rebuild us even stronger.

Sometimes He has to knock you down to remind you He is God, and you are not. Many times though, you knock yourself down, and while you are weeping on your knees, wallowing in the dust that was just created, He is doing a glorious work in your heart. He is creating beauty from ashes. He is waiting for you to crawl into His arms and rest in His peace and stillness.

With Him, no moment of brokenness is wasted.

Your life is beautiful, but each day our Father is crafting it into something even better.

Day in and day out, I am unintentionally trying to fill that role of perfection the world has put on me, and without knowing it, I am stripping myself of the sheer joy, peace, and stillness our Father created us to have as a part of our life.

I allow the voices of perfection to run my world, rather than letting His truth fill my mind.

He tells me His strength is made perfect in my weakness. That in my weakness He can perform His greatest miracles. That in my imperfection, His Kingdom is built.

My Father never told me I was going to act perfect. Instead, He told me I was perfectly made.

Perfectly made in His image to be refined and built up over time to reflect Him. Being perfectly made isn't something we have to strive to be, it's just who we are. It doesn't take work because He's already taken care of it all.

*"And in him you too are **being** built together to become a dwelling in which God lives by his Spirit."*

Ephesians 2:22

BEING PERFECTLY MADE
ISN'T SOMETHING WE
HAVE TO STRIVE TO BE,
IT'S JUST WHO WE ARE.

He doesn't expect me to live a perfect life. Actually, He promised me I would mess up. I would fail. I would fall short. I would be put in moments of struggle and temptation. I would be human, and that He would be God.

He is telling you the same thing.

He sent His Son to die for you, to die for me, so our imperfect choices could be forgiven, redeemed, and covered in grace.

So, if it's a guarantee I can't act perfect, maybe it's time I stop trying. After all, my Father tells me it is not about seeking the approval of man, but rather living a life that honors Him. He tells me that in this world I will have trouble, but He has already overcome that trouble for me. I only need to rest in Him.

"Obviously, I'm not trying to win the approval of people, but of God. If pleasing people were my goal, I would not be Christ's servant."

Galatians 1:10 (NLT)

"I have told you these things, so that in me you may have peace. In this world you will have trouble. But take heart! I have overcome the world."

John 16:33

I am not perfect, but I am perfectly made.

My life is not perfect, but the One who created life is.

I am not unbreakable, but He fits all the broken pieces together.

I can't be everything and do everything, but His strength is made perfect in my weakness.

So, I will continue to be imperfect, and proud of it, because in my imperfection He shines. In my imperfection, He does His greatest work. In my imperfection, He wraps His arms around me and covers me in His unconditional boundless love.

Letting my Father do the heavy lifting, which He has already promised He will do for me, is far better than attempting to live up to a standard of perfection the world has put on me. Living life rooted in His peace is the best life to live.

The first step of surrender is recognizing how much we need our Father and how bound we are without Him. When we can surrender the desire and attempt to fill a role of perfection we can't live up to, it will bring a rest that can only come from Him.

I am not perfect; instead, I rest in my perfect Savior.

Take a Minute

Remember

- We are not called to do "us"; we are called to model "Him."
- Our imperfect humanness doesn't affect His ability to be a perfect Father.
- The truth is the world won't just push us to our breaking point, it will push us over the edge. It's up to us not to let it.
- While the world will never be silent, neither will our Father. His truth will never be void. His voice will always have the power to speak louder.
- With Him, no moment of brokenness is wasted.
- Being perfectly made isn't something we have to strive to be, it's just who we are.

Recite

"You are the light of the world. A town built on a hill cannot be hidden. Neither do people light a lamp and put it under a bowl. Instead, they put it on its stand, and it gives light to everyone in the house. In the same way, let your light shine before others, that they may see your good deeds and glorify your Father in heaven."

Matthew 5:14-16

"For you created my inmost being; you knit me together in my mother's womb. I praise you because I am fearfully and wonderfully made; your works are wonderful, I know that full well."

Psalm 139:13-14

"So God created mankind in his own image, in the image of God he created them; male and female he created them."

Genesis 1:27

"The mind governed by the flesh is death, but the mind governed by the Spirit is life and peace."

Romans 8:6

*"And in him you too are **being** built together to become a dwelling in which God lives by his Spirit."*

Ephesians 2:22

"Obviously, I'm not trying to win the approval of people, but of God. If pleasing people were my goal, I would not be Christ's servant."

Galatians 1:10 (NLT)

"I have told you these things, so that in me you may have peace. In this world you will have trouble. But take heart! I have overcome the world."

John 16:33

Reflect

- Have you ever felt paralyzed by the words used to describe you? If so, what were they? How did those words make you feel?
- Describe a time you found yourself striving to uphold a reputation given to you by someone else or even by yourself?
- Do you believe you were created with perfection and intention?
- In your life, who is an image bearer of our Heavenly Father?
- "I am not perfect; instead, I rest in my perfect Savior." What would resting in Him look like for you?

Respond

Take a few minutes to talk with God about what is stirring in your heart. Tell Him what expectations you feel paralyzed by and then ask Him to help you find release and freedom from them. Thank Him for creating you with intention and perfection and then ask Him how you can better reflect Him to this world. And finally, sit in His presence and ask Him who He says you are. Take the first step of surrender by laying down the lies of the world and resting in the truth of who He created you to be.

Chapter two

rooted in trust

rooted in trust

Did you ever play the game MASH when you were a kid? You made a list of all the different parts you thought made up an adult life...who you were married to, what your career was, how many kids you had, what state you lived in, what your salary was, what kind of house you owned, and it went on and on. You would list out all these options for each category and then through various techniques you would come up with a number. You would then use the number to go through and eliminate options until there was only one remaining for each category. In a matter of minutes, you had your whole future planned out.

Sometimes, the game was in your favor, and you would end the game imagining yourself married to the cutest kid in the school. Maybe you ended up with the biggest salary, lived in a mansion, and had three children. It sounded like the perfect life.

Other times, your friend cackled while you were thankful it was just a game because by the end you were predicted to live in a shack, marry the weirdest kid in your grade, have twelve kids, and clean toilets for a living.

Everyone knew you couldn't really find out how your future was going to turn out, but you were still set on trying to figure it out.

MASH is the best way I can sum up my childhood. It was years of planning and dreaming up the perfect future for myself.

I was going to attend Denver University and room with my best friend. We had our colors already picked out for our dorm room. Then, I planned to meet the man of my dreams while in college and get married when I was 21 (that was my favorite number growing up). I was going to be a teacher and eventually transition to being a stay-at-home mom. I started off wanting twelve kids and over time I became wiser until I landed on wanting six kids. I had the genders, age gaps, and names all picked out. I also had a floor plan of my future home in a laminated sleeve to keep it safe. My dream home was a *tiny* bit extravagant…the floor plan included a fountain in the entryway.

I literally had my whole life planned out. Most of the plan came to me easily, but the part I always struggled deciding on was the name of my future husband. For some reason, I had a tough time figuring that out up front.

While this "game" naturally should have ended once I got a little older and understood life a bit more, it didn't stop for me. I became a tad more realistic about life, but my obsession with planning my future didn't end. Even so, over and over again, my perfectly mapped out ideas kept failing.

When deciding on colleges, I vowed I wouldn't go more than forty-five minutes away from home.

I ended up going twenty-two hours away to a school in Tennessee.

The summer before my freshman year of college, I told my girlfriends I was sure I would have a boyfriend by Christmas break, which would have been in December of 2013.

It is now July of 2020 and I have yet to have had a boyfriend (yes, you read that correctly).

I was planning to graduate, move home, and teach at the school I had grown up attending.

I got a job offer at that school but ended up taking a job at another school I hadn't even considered prior to the interview.

When beginning the search to buy a home, I said I would never buy something without seeing it first.

A week later I bought a place I hadn't even stepped foot in while I was hundreds of miles away exploring Yellowstone.

As you can see, my life is a series of *my* well thought out, well intended plans, never really coming to fruition.

And PRAISE GOD for that!

My plans were based on what I knew at that moment. His plans are based on my past, my present, and my future.

My plans are based on my emotions and earthly desires. His plans are based on the truth that He knows all, He sees all, and He loves me.

My plans are self-serving. His plans are Kingdom building.

Here's what it boils down to: The life I am living right now is not what I had planned. My life is surprising to me. It is not at all how I pictured it looking. But man-oh-man, it is the best life and so perfectly crafted by my Father.

As I sit here writing this, I am 25 years old.

If I would have predicted what my life would look like at 25, here's what I would have said...I would be married to the man of my dreams entering my fifth year of teaching.

Instead, in this exact moment, I am nowhere close to getting married and I am preparing to tell my school I won't be returning next year so I can go work full time in the church.

————

MY PLANS ARE SELF-SERVING.
HIS PLANS ARE KINGDOM BUILDING.

————

Yep, the difference between my plans and His plans are astronomical.

• • •

For many years it wasn't a relationship of trust I had with God, but rather one where I fought for control. I thought that through my prayers I was fervently seeking Him and His will. I soon learned, through His kindness and gentleness, I wasn't seeking His will, but instead trying to force my wishful will for my life upon Him.

I learned while prayer has the power to change my life and the lives of others, the heart behind a prayer is what matters most.

All my life, the people around me prayed, so it became a part of my life at a young age. I prayed for those who were sick, for a math test I had the next day, or in the moments when I felt hurt by a friend. They were simple prayers lifted up by a child and were lovingly heard and received by my Father. For many years, there was never anything urgent I needed to pray for. No massive requests or heartbreaking situations I was going through, and all my prayers were answered the way I would have expected. It made prayer a very simple, fundamental, logical way to approach life.

Growing up I developed a list I prayed over. When someone was in need, I attached their name to the end of my list I recited each night before bed. Over time, my list got incredibly long, and I got ridiculously fast at saying it. There were times I prayed through the list so quickly no one could understand it and honestly, I couldn't even tell you what I was saying. But you better believe I was proud of my list, how long it was, and that I had it memorized.

Over the years, I got good at giving God lists of things I wanted Him to take care of. It seemed to work fine.

But that all changed.

In May of 2012 when my sweet grandpa (we called him Fuzzy) was diagnosed with stage four esophageal cancer, it was the first big hit I had ever experienced. It was the first time I felt real fear about losing someone. As we learned more about the cancer and how much it had invaded his body, the reality set in of the fight that was about to go down, and the chance he had of winning.

I remember the night after I found out, I prayed for healing, but I also begged my Father to protect my faith through this. I knew it was in moments like this – moments full of uncertainty, fear, and potential heartbreak – the devil was on the prowl. I was determined to not make any space for his lies to seep in. I had watched too many people lose their faith in times like this. I knew I couldn't survive without my faith, so it was vital it be the strongest it's ever been.

For six months my family prayed and fought alongside Fuzzy, but on October 25, 2012, our sweet, strong, and loyal grandpa went to be with Jesus.

Initially, I felt relief. Relief the fight was over, and he was free of pain. Then, I felt sadness as I realized the massive hole that was now left in our family. After that, it turned into frustration and anger at our Father for not healing Fuzzy in the way we had been praying for – and suddenly Matthew 7:7 became a big lie to me.

"Ask and it will be given to you…"

For the first time ever, what I asked for was not given to me, and my heart was shattered. The Bible – this Book of truth – didn't seem like it was all truth…

And so, I wrestled. I sought guidance from others, I prayed, and I read up on this piece of Scripture, but I could not figure out why my Father would tell me that whatever I asked for He would give me when the biggest prayer of my life was just ignored.

Eventually, I became sick of fighting. I knew my Father was good, and so I stuffed my feelings deep down and just kept living life. I just decided the Bible was *mostly* truth and that was good enough for me. It was a scary thought, but I wasn't sure what other option I had. I loved God, believed in Him, His goodness, and His Word, but I didn't know how to sort through this disappointment in my life. He had let me down and I didn't know what to do with that.

Have you ever felt this way?

After my grandpa died, I began to pray for health and safety every morning over my family. I had this deep-rooted fear that if for one day I didn't pray this prayer, a family member was going to end up getting sick or getting hurt. I felt such immense pressure to keep everyone alive – daily – with my prayers. I believed my words and desires held that much weight.

Four years later I was listening to a podcast series on prayer and was in the middle of training for a half marathon. It was five in the morning and as I was running and listening, my Father revealed something to me that changed everything.

He told me that when I prayed, it was out of fear and gaining a sense of control. That rather than putting the power of prayer in the hands of the One I prayed to, I was attempting to put the power in my hands believing my words were what really mattered. He assured me it was His job to care for His children, not mine, and that rather than making prayer a burden in my life, He desired for it to be something that brought freedom.

As He reminded me of His power, His strength, His perfect will, and His insane love for His children, I realized how little credit I had been giving Him. Me, a simple child who knew so little, had been using prayer as a way to try and dictate to God the things I wanted, believing that was how it should work.

But in His most gracious loving way, He revealed to me not only my inadequacy to dictate to Him what needed to happen, but also the lack of need to do this.

That instead of being brought lists of wishes and demands, He desires to be a refuge for His children. A safe place. A place of freedom and peace. A place where we come for rest.

That when we come to Him, we aren't coming from a place of fear and a need for control, but rather an intimate knowledge of who He is.

He is good. He knows all. He sees all. He has our best interests in mind, and He adores us.

And in knowing all this, fear dissolves and is replaced with unexplainable trust and faith in His character and His plan.

In that moment, my Father was offering me a life of freedom. One where I can come to Him at all moments of the day, with anything, in any condition, with any feeling, and pour out my heart to Him in complete surrender knowing He will take care of it all.

Rather than a prayer life dictated by fear, He desires for us to adopt a prayer life rooted in trust.

A prayer life where we surrender everything to Him, and then wait expectantly for what He is going to do.

"In the morning, Lord, You hear my voice; in the morning I lay my requests before you and wait expectantly."

Psalm 5:3

This is what He desires for us to do; bring Him anything and everything, at all moments of the day or night, with any worry, joy, or frustration, eager to see what He will do with it.

"Ask and it will be given to you..."

I see now where my misunderstanding was. Our Father isn't saying, "Ask for whatever *you* want and what *you* believe is best," but rather He says, "bring it all to Me, pray for My will, and trust I will take care of it".

As I was coming to understand this, I wrote down what I felt the Lord saying to me. *"Come to Me with your dreams, hopes, and desires, but then offer it all up to Me knowing My will and My plan for your life is the one that will stand and come to fruition."*

"Many are the plans in the mind of a man, but it is the purpose of the Lord that will stand."

Proverbs 19:21 (ESV)

I think of my second-grade students and the way they always came to me. Whether they needed their shoelace unknotted, needed help spelling a word, had hurt feelings, or had an unsafe home…they would come to me with no filter and no fear, trusting I would take care of their problem because they knew I loved them. They trusted me to take care of them. They believed I knew their needs and would provide for them.

Our Father is no different. He desires for us to come to Him, trusting in Him, resting in His love, and surrendering all things to Him, eager for what He will do.

• • •

I know – without any doubt – that He will provide for you financially. He will restore your broken relationships. He will make your next step clear. He will grant you patience. He will comfort you in times of sadness. He will tend to your every need.

This is a prayer life rooted in trust. This is what a relationship with our Father looks like that is built on the assurance and belief He is good, He loves you, and He will care for you.

But trust isn't always easy. It doesn't always come naturally. Sometimes, we have to fight for it.

If there is one thing I have learned in life, it is that I desperately want to trust my Father because life without the peace of knowing and believing He has it all figured out for me is no good at all.

Living a life where I believe my future and even the future of others is in my realm of control is too much. It becomes too overwhelming and over time, in an effort to make myself feel more able, I begin to become self-righteous and focus more on my efforts and results rather than submitting to His will and basking in the goodness that comes from it.

He sees you. He sees your needs. He hears your requests.

Believe it or not, and whether you see it or not, He is working on your behalf right now. He is moving mountains and changing hearts to create a life that is perfectly crafted to suit you. He has not forgotten you. He has not abandoned you. He is in complete control. Trust that.

This life of true surrender and a prayer life rooted in trust can be scary, because when you ask for His will, He will ask big things of you.

He will ask you to throw out that laminated sleeve with your well thought-out, well-intentioned plans, and step out into the fog where you can only see one step at a time.

And that's where I currently am in life and it's where I've been for a while…in a fog. Completely unaware of where I am headed, but slowly gaining sight of the next step in front of me while trying my best to trust and take each leap as it comes.

Let me start back at the beginning of my fog so you can truly grasp the work my Father has been doing in my heart and the seeds He has been planting in me for so long.

At the beginning of every year, I ask God to give me a word – one that speaks to the epic plan He has for that year of my life. A word that provides me with a sense of boldness and guidance for what the next 365 days will hold.

On January 7th, 2019, this was my prayer…

> *For this next year I feel You placing the word **ANTICIPATE** on my heart…that word makes me so excited. I feel like You are calling me to excitedly anticipate what You will do with me this year, what You will give me, and what I will experience. I feel led to pray for big things with anticipation, trusting and knowing You are going to move in big ways.*

Now, if I stopped the prayer right there, you might think, "Wow, it's amazing how in tune she is with what our Father was saying to her in that moment." You might get this idea that I always have a clear sense of clarity and vision.

Unfortunately, that isn't true for me and really it isn't true for any of us. We can and will spend our whole lives trying to be better at hearing the voice of God. At having discernment to hear His voice only. In those moments where we are trying to listen, we must learn to eliminate our own voice and the voices of others around us.

We don't always hear clearly, but if we keep seeking, eventually we gain clarity.

Here is the rest of that prayer…

> *And this may be totally insane and I am a little nervous to put this in writing, but I just feel like You are going to pull through this year and bring me my husband…that sounds insane but I just have this feeling You are telling me to excitedly anticipate how You are going to pull through on that this year…continue to lead my heart in wisdom with this. I want to hear You correctly.*

41

Even then, I knew I might have been putting some of my own desires and wishful plans into His words for me. I knew well enough to pray for clarity and I worked to continue to seek what He was wanting me to anticipate. Where He was calling me to lean, seek, and discover.

The testimony of His faithfulness in the continued search for my husband is one I will share with you, but not right now.

Right now, I want to focus on this idea of anticipation He placed on my heart in January of 2019. This incredible story of His will for my life slowly being revealed to me while He simultaneously did a crazy, wild, and wonderful work in my heart.

I want you to see the way He so gently began to mold and change my heart. I want you to see the confusion I experienced while trying to gain clarity and the raw and real work He did in me. The best way I can do that is by giving you a glimpse into my conversations with Him. These are some of the prayers I wrote throughout 2019 while crying out to God for clarity in feeling this sense that something was coming...

July 25, 2019

I'm thirsty to lead people...through worship, writing, speaking...I'm thirsty to influence Your people and speak truth into their lives. But I don't know what steps to take or what direction to head. I don't know if there should be something I'm pursuing...I just don't know. Show me, Father. Show me if there are steps I need to take. I want to follow.

September 1, 2019

Father, I feel like You have big things in store for me, and I want to be ready. Continue to speak to me. Use me. Mold me.

September 13, 2019

So much to say…so much on my heart. Deep down for ten years I have been harboring this dream of being a worship leader at a church. I've imagined it for years but never really told anyone. It all started when Sherri told me she had a vision of me being on stage leading others in worship. Not even one year ago I joined worship at Journey. I went in unsure of it all, unsure of my ability, but You have blown my mind. I have never felt more in Your will than when I am on stage. Here's the other piece of it. I feel like my heart for others, caring for them, and reaching out has grown immensely and it is shocking to me. The idea behind ministry – to invest in others – is suddenly becoming so intriguing. I don't know, God. All I know is I feel like I am sitting on a ticking time bomb…that my 2019 word of "anticipate" couldn't be more true. I don't know what to expect, but I'm excited. I simply want to walk in Your will, so please open and shut doors. Thank You for using me.

November 18, 2019

Father, these last few months with writing and worship, I just feel so sure something is coming. I absolutely love encouraging others and speaking Your truth through writing and worship. Please open up doors of opportunity for me. Help me to be obedient to Your voice. Speak to me. Show me how I can serve You with my time, talents, and money…I love You.

December 2, 2019

As I began praying about Advent, it is all about waiting on You. The obvious one is waiting for my husband. I feel silly I wrote that I felt like You would bring Him to me this year. I feel like that word "ANTICIPATE" is still accurate even though nothing ever came of it…because not only do I feel like I'm sitting anticipating my husband, but I'm also doing it with worship and writing. I feel like You have opened big doors and I can't see where all of it is leading...I trust You fully. Help me to continue to seek You.

Every time I read those prayers I am astounded.

It's unreal to me to look back and see His hand over everything. In the moments where we feel like He is absent, He is actually moving mountains and transforming our hearts so everything will align just the way He planned. Our Father is never absent, if anything, He is present in more ways than we ever thought possible.

We just have to seek Him. And when we do, we will find Him and realize He has been right beside us this whole time.

But it's important to remember that He may not be working in the way we think He is. I always want to "figure God out." I try to predict where His plan is going or why He did something but doing that has always led to frustration because I can never get it right. Ultimately, He is working in every area of our lives for the sake of His Kingdom and our heart, but it will most likely look different than what we were envisioning, and we have to be okay with that.

The more we get to know God and His character, the easier it becomes to trust what we can't see or understand. The peace and joy come regardless of the outcome.

OUR FATHER IS NEVER ABSENT,
IF ANYTHING, HE IS
PRESENT IN MORE WAYS THAN
WE EVER THOUGHT POSSIBLE.

Now, I can think of only a few times in my life where I prayed for God's guidance and honestly wanted it.

Anyone else feel me on this?

I am so guilty of praying for His guidance when really all I want is His blessing on the plan I already have laid out for myself.

I want my fairy godfather to use His wand and make the plans I have written and placed in my laminated sleeve become a reality. Right then and right there. Bippity boppity boo.

It's that desire for control. All humans want it. We THINK it makes us feel safe and secure. We BELIEVE it is how we can live happily ever after filled with peace.

I prayed for God's will with my grandpa when he got diagnosed with cancer, but really, I just wanted Him to follow through on my plan to heal my grandpa here on earth. And when He didn't follow my plan, I felt betrayed and confused.

After that, I went through a season of truly clinging to prayer as my outlet to control my life and the lives of those around me. I began to feel as though God was my puppet, and my words were guiding His footsteps.

How foolish of me.

Living a life filled with prayers vying for control only led to disappointment, frustration, and feelings of angst. I felt as though I was holding the whole world on my shoulders. I believed it all depended on my words and the things I brought to our Father. The sense of control I believed would fill me with peace and security, only made me feel unsettled and unsure about everything. It was the most uneasy I had ever felt.

Because in that season, rather than recognizing the King of Kings was over it all, I put myself in charge. Rather than resting in the shadow of His wings, I attempted to find refuge in the security of my plan.

Prayer has the power to produce a life of freedom, peace, and joy. It has the power to grow and nurture an incredibly beautiful and intimate relationship with our Father. It has the power to transform our heart, but in order for all of this to happen, we must take the right approach.

"When you ask, you do not receive, because you ask with wrong motives, that you may spend what you get on your pleasures."

James 4:3

"This is the confidence we have in approaching God: that if we ask anything according to his will, he hears us."

1 John 5:14

"Pray then like this: 'Our Father in heaven, hallowed be your name. Your kingdom come, your will be done, on earth as it is in heaven. Give us this day our daily bread, and forgive us our debts, as we also have forgiven our debtors. And lead us not into temptation, but deliver us from evil.'"

Matthew 6:9-13 (ESV)

Jesus taught us to pray asking for our Father's will.

Prayer is most powerful when we approach our Father not only asking for His guidance, but also truly surrendering our own plans and desires.

When we come to Him with hands open wide, emptied of ourselves, ready to be filled with His leading, transformation happens, and lives are changed. That is when His Kingdom is built, and He does a wild work within your heart.

Prayer must be coupled with surrender.

Naturally, surrender is uncomfortable. It leaves us feeling vulnerable, exposed, and lost. But our Father doesn't ask us to surrender it all and stand there naked and afraid. No way. Instead, He scoops us up in our most desperate and helpless state, and He fills our empty hands with His good and perfect plan for us. He overwhelms us with His peace, His joy, His truth, and His grace. He equips and empowers us to keep in step with Him and build His Kingdom.

PRAYER MUST BE
COUPLED WITH SURRENDER.

2019 was a year of preparation for me. My Father began a work in my heart where I wasn't just seeking guidance in hopes of approval for my life plan, but rather I began to grow this longing for truly seeking and knowing His will for me. I was no longer in search of a way to fulfill my desires, but instead I recognized there was this deep longing in my heart for something greater. My heart desired to know His will, not mine.

So instead of praying to gain control and make plans, I just began to pray He would reveal His will to me, and until then, that He would refine and renew my heart to be ready for what was next.

For the first time ever, my hands were open wide in surrender in search of what He wanted to fill them with.

I realized my laminated sleeves that held my future plans were no longer my bible. They were not my truth. They did not get to dictate my course.

Rather than letting a game – like my childhood game of MASH – tell me where I was headed, I asked the Creator of the universe to show me my next step.

I felt this prompting in my heart that something was coming, and I needed to be ready.

And this is where we need to anchor ourselves – desperately seeking His will for us in the midst of life's unknowns. We must decide the peace that comes from living in the unknown isn't a peace that comes from within us, but it's a peace that comes from our Father who promises us He is holding us in the palm of His hands, gently molding our heart, and revealing His will to us one step at a time.

"Come to me, all you who are weary and burdened, and I will give you rest."

Matthew 11:28

This truth brings me such joy.

I picture us (you and me) attempting to carry the weight of the world on our shoulders sinking closer and closer to the ground with each step while the feelings of being tired and exhausted and overwhelmed begin to suffocate us. I imagine us trying to make big strides to keep going in this race of life, but in all reality, we are not gaining any ground. We are stagnant and losing the will to fight.

And all while we are so focused on the race in front of us, losing with each next step, burdened by the things we have taken upon ourselves, our Father is standing right next to us with His hands wide open offering us a weightless ride.

He sees our struggle. He sees our desire to do it on our own. He knows our love for control. He was the One who created us.

So, He stands there, and He waits. While we struggle with each step, He continually whispers, *"My child, you can stop now. You don't have to do it alone. I see where you are headed, and I will show you how to get there. Stop demanding you do this on your own. You were designed to need Me. Come, find rest."*

And finally, in 2020, I did just that. Rather than carrying my life on my shoulders, I gave it all to Him and opened my hands wide.

He asked me to take a leap, and I did. My plans were about to crumble all around me…

Father, I surrender it all to You.

Your will, not mine.

Show me where to go.

RATHER THAN
A PRAYER LIFE DICTATED
BY FEAR, HE DESIRES FOR
US TO ADOPT A PRAYER
LIFE ROOTED IN TRUST.

Take a Minute

Remember

- My plans are self-serving. His plans are Kingdom building.
- Rather than a prayer life dictated by fear, He desires for us to adopt a prayer life rooted in trust.
- He is moving mountains and changing hearts to create a life that is perfectly crafted to suit you.
- When you ask for His will, He will ask big things of you.
- The more we get to know God and His character, the easier it becomes to trust what we can't see or understand.
- Prayer must be coupled with surrender.

Recite

"Ask and it will be given to you…"

Matthew 7:7

"In the morning, Lord, You hear my voice; in the morning I lay my requests before you and wait expectantly."

Psalm 5:3

"Many are the plans in the mind of a man, but it is the purpose of the Lord that will stand."

Proverbs 19:21 (ESV)

"When you ask, you do not receive, because you ask with wrong motives, that you may spend what you get on your pleasures."

James 4:3

"This is the confidence we have in approaching God: that if we ask anything according to his will, he hears us."

1 John 5:14

"Pray then like this: 'Our Father in heaven, hallowed be your name. Your kingdom come, your will be done, on earth as it is in heaven. Give us this day our daily bread, and forgive us our debts, as we also have forgiven our debtors. And lead us not into temptation, but deliver us from evil.'"

Matthew 6:9-13 (ESV)

"Come to me, all you who are weary and burdened, and I will give you rest."

Matthew 11:28

Reflect

- What plans have you written for your life that haven't worked out?
- Take inventory of your life as it is right now. Is this what you had planned or predicted for yourself?
- Describe a time you prayed really hard for something, and it didn't go the way you wanted. How did it impact your faith and how you viewed God?
- What questions or doubts do you have about God that you have been ignoring?

- What role has prayer played in your life before today?
- Do you trust God (completely)?

Respond

Take a few minutes to talk with God about what is stirring in your heart. Are you frustrated with where He has brought you, or are you filled with gratitude? Do you feel discouraged when you think about the wounds in your life? If you do, tell Him. Tell Him exactly what you feel. Ask Him the hard questions. He can handle it. And then take a minute to sit in His presence and reflect on how you have approached prayer in your life. Ask Him to show you how your prayer life can be rooted in trust rather than fear.

Chapter three

fighting for surrender

fighting for surrender

I love to think back to my first few days of 2020. There was so much talk over the idea of a new decade. Looking back on the last ten years of your life, reflecting, and then looking forward while hoping, dreaming, and planning what the next ten years of life will hold.

I am a sucker for all things "New Year's." Reading the prayers I had written and things I had learned in the past year always fill me with joy. I love reflecting on the last 365 days and seeing the incredible ways He has worked in my life and the lives of those around me; and I love looking forward and seeking His guidance on the next year and how I can grow and honor Him more.

Can I go on a little tangent for just a minute?

I need to tell you that one of the most powerful things you can do for yourself is to begin writing down your prayers. Our thoughts are often fleeting, but our Father asks us to pray expectantly. He desires for us to reflect on the ways He has worked in our life. He wants our answered prayers to bring Him glory. All too often, we offer up a prayer to Him, forget about it, and when He answers the prayer, we don't even notice.

Writing down our prayers gives us a chance to come back and remember the requests we brought to Him and see His faithfulness in all of it.

It allows us the chance to be reminded of the way He hears us, see the way He is working in our hearts, and it creates an incredible testimony to how faithful He is in hearing and answering our prayers.

Your prayers don't need to be fancy. They don't need to be long. They don't need to be anything other than the unedited, unfiltered outpouring of your heart. He already knows your every thought, so let loose and rest in His unconditional love for you. Just talk to Him. I promise it is worth it.

Okay, back to my original thought.

2020 started off with prayers full of praise for His faithfulness and goodness in 2019 and prayers full of expectation and excitement for what 2020 would bring. From the beginning I was crying out to Him for guidance, asking that He would make His will clear to me. I was doing my best to truly lay it all at His feet. I found myself still stuck on the word "anticipate" and was anxiously awaiting the moment the clouds would part and everything would make sense (if only life worked that way…).

I started my annual 21 days of prayer and fasting and on the morning of January 6 I was doing my best to set the tone and intention for the next 21 days and focus my heart on what I was hoping to learn.

January 6, 2020

Father, I have felt that from last year I still have so many unmet expectations, hopes, and prayers but I keep hearing You telling me to keep praying on it, to keep waiting expectantly and to continue anticipating what You will do. Father, where do I need to make changes or move in a different direction? Open my heart to be refined and to hear You clearly.

Later that day I wrote this prayer.

Father, I'm actually nervous to write this, but I just continue to feel this draw towards ministry...open and close doors, give me clarity.

Two days later our church had a night of worship and prayer and He whispered to me that I needed to talk to someone about working at the church.

I don't know about you, but I have learned that when the Holy Spirit prompts me, I need to act fast before I wimp out.

"If you love me, you will keep my commandments. And I will ask the Father, and he will give you another Helper, to be with you forever, even the Spirit of truth, whom the world cannot receive, because it neither sees him nor knows him. You know him, for he dwells with you and will be in you."

John 14:15-17 (ESV)

Before I share with you how I responded that day, I want to revisit what I talked about in an earlier chapter – the importance of knowing His voice amidst the noise of this world.

Our own thoughts, the opinions of this world, the distractions that surround us, they all clamor relentlessly for our attention and if we don't learn to silence them, to allow His voice be heard above the rest, we are going to miss out on so much the Holy Spirit has to offer us.

We must create space and opportunity to hear Him. The world won't go silent for us, so we must silence it ourselves. This means putting down our phones, opening up His Word, putting on worship music, sitting in His presence...it means intentional moments of desiring to meet with Him and hear Him.

In His goodness and love for us, with Jesus no longer physically on earth, God knew we needed a helper. He knew we needed someone who, at any moment, could help guide us and speak truth into us. Our Father desires for us to hear His voice clearly, so the Holy Spirit came to dwell within us.

THE WORLD WON'T GO SILENT FOR US,
SO WE MUST SILENCE IT OURSELVES.

To dwell within our broken, twisted, and deceitful hearts and bring light.

This is a true gift of love.

Through continued discipline and experience, through intentional prayer and intentional times of silence, we slowly learn how to hear from the Holy Spirit and discern that voice above the rest.

And if you are anything like me, when prompted by the Holy Spirit, it is often something that makes your heart skip a beat. I know I am hearing from the Holy Spirit when a thought or gut feeling comes in such a strong wave, I can't pretend it didn't happen. Normally it is something that brings up immediate feelings of fear or trepidation. It is always something out of my comfort zone and something I never would have come up with on my own.

Simply put, it is a leading that is clearly from the King Himself.

It can't be ignored. No matter how hard you try it can't be forgotten. And it strengthens you by reminding you of past successful experiences with the power of God's grace, guiding you to be brave one more time.

Too many times in my life I have heard and not acted. Out of fear, embarrassment, or uncertainty, I decided I was going to try and disregard His leading and as a result, I know I have missed an opportunity.

While I wish I had been obedient to every whisper, I know in my imperfect human state and trajectory of continual growth, those missed opportunities were still moments of learning what it's like to hear His voice.

I won't ever be perfect at it, but I hope that with each passing day my ability to discern His voice strengthens and my obedience in following His leading increases.

I hope the same thing for you.

That as you continue to create space for Him to speak to you, you will hear Him more often, and have the boldness and courage to act on His leading.

The longer we sit on His prompting, the easier it is to talk ourselves out of obedience.

I've heard it said this way - when the enemy can delay us, he can get ahold of us.

———

THE LONGER WE SIT ON HIS PROMPTING,
THE EASIER IT IS TO TALK OURSELVES
OUT OF OBEDIENCE.

———

And he's not the only stumbling block. The ways of the world, and often the ways of our human heart, will speak to all the reasons we shouldn't be obedient. Those voices will feed the fear, anxiety, or pride that all too often stop us from following through. We can't let that happen.

We must intentionally listen for His voice, and once we hear it, we then must act on it.

> *"Do not merely listen to the word, and so deceive yourselves. Do what it says. Anyone who listens to the word but does not do what it says is like someone who looks at his face in a mirror and, after looking at himself, goes away and immediately forgets what he looks like. But whoever looks intently into the perfect law that gives freedom, and continues in it—not forgetting what they have heard, but doing it—they will be blessed in what they do."*

> James 1:22-25

Now, back to the worship night and the Holy Spirit's whispered guidance. Knowing He was speaking clearly to me, before I even had time to convince myself I heard wrong, I reached out to someone at church. I told them I had no idea what I was even thinking, but that God told me to talk to them about working at the church.

And then it all happened really fast. Conversations with people at church began to take place and suddenly I realized there might be real opportunity for me to step into full-time ministry. This was no longer some distant thought I'd written in my prayer journal, but actual guidance from the Holy Spirit.

January 14, 2020

Father, I'm not feeling super centered during this time like I wanted to. I feel a bit all over the place. I really want to gain clarity from You. I want to hear from You. Thanks for loving me and choosing me.

January 20, 2020

Father, this whole thing scares me a bit, but in the end, You are sovereign and good and I trust You. You told me 13 months ago to anticipate…so here I am praying for Your will.

January 21, 2020

Father, my heart is feeling so many things. The thought of leaving teaching breaks my heart but stepping into a new avenue of Your will for me is really exciting. My gut tells me one thing…it's hard to imagine You leading me here for it to just stop, but You also could be working in my life in other capacities. Give me wisdom. Show me the way You want me to go because I will follow.

January 24, 2020

Father, I realize when I began praying the big prayer of "I am Yours, I surrender it all to You, I will go where You call me," it would open up doors that might be scary. This would be a huge leap of faith, but You call us to trust You, to not lean on our own understanding, and to just follow You one step at a time. Continue to lead me…I'm listening.

Through conversation with several leaders, and a lot of prayer, the church leadership team began to piece together a role for me.

February 14, 2020

Father, I'm feeling overwhelmed. I feel like I dreamed about working at the church for a while and was excited. Now, the opportunity is right here and it's overwhelming because an actual decision has to be made — no more dreaming. Yesterday I was begging You for guidance and then this thought came to mind — whether it was from me or You I don't quite know…

Morgan, you want guidance? I have been telling you for the last 13 months that something was coming. I have been telling you to anticipate and that I wanted to use you. I've been telling you to wait because something was coming. Then, I show you what it is, and I ask you to move on it. When you do, the church immediately opens up their doors, wanting you on their team, and then things shift at school for next year. Is that not enough Morgan? Do you need more than that?

And just like that I knew what was happening, but I still wasn't willing to fully admit to it.

God called me out on the fact that I had all the answers right in front of me, yet I wasn't willing to let that be enough. I still acted and prayed like He was leaving me high and dry with no answers or guidance.

Really, I was just too scared to let what was happening be enough to make me feel confident and at peace with the idea that this was the change I needed to make in my life.

The church creating a position for me and things shifting at school for the next year SHOULD have been enough, but I was asking God for more. I needed more proof this was actually what He was saying to me.

February 27, 2020

Father, I'm over here trying to be chill and trust…I'm even having a hard time writing because my mind is moving so fast. This is all starting to get so real and I'm starting to get really freaked out. Should I really leave a job I love and am good at? I would be leaving something good for the unknown…Is this really where You want me to go? I will follow but I've lost a bit of the gumption to really feel like this is You. Please give me a little more guidance…

It's always…"God, please, just a little more guidance. Just one more sure sign this is what You are saying to me."

Well friends, guess what, as my story will continue to show, sometimes no matter the clarity He gives you, the number of "signs" He gives you, or what He says to you, eventually you just have to take the leap.

When He asks us to do scary things it isn't always smooth. It doesn't always just fall into place. It doesn't always or really ever feel easy.

Because what He calls us to is against the ways of the world and often against our human nature of always wanting to be comfortable.

He calls us to live by faith. To live in the unknown. To take risks for Him. To follow His leading even when it seems foggy.

He never said following Him would be easy.

In Luke 9:23, Jesus said, *"Whoever wants to be my disciple must deny themselves and take up their cross daily and follow me."*

DAILY.

It is a daily decision to choose to follow Him. To take the risks. To step into the unknown.

We must set aside our comforts daily. We must fight each day to live for Him.

A sure sign or word from Him may bring clarity in the moment, but the fog might return the next morning, so we must take one step at a time – deeper into the fog – knowing His light will guide each step.

March 7, 2020

It's almost as though my word for 2020 is surrender. That is truly at the heart of what I am feeling. A surrender of it all — living in the grey area — and learning to be okay with it. In the last two months You have broken me down to my core. I'm completely exposed, but I've never felt stronger. I've desired You and relied on You like never before. I have felt the enemy attack me on all ends, but Your Word and Your truth stands.

Surrender.

Here it really was. This moment where everything changed for me. Where I realized what was actually happening in my life.

My plans were falling apart.

The life I had envisioned for myself. The life I had so carefully planned out. It had crumbled and vanished.

My heart had been shattered in the last few months with a brutal reminder of how broken our world is, and my heart had done a 360 in terms of where I felt called.

I was exhausted. I felt weak. I felt vulnerable. I felt out of control.

And at the same time, I felt more peace and authentic joy than I'd ever felt before.

It was like this freedom had washed over me when I decided to let go.

Rather than gripping my fists as tightly as possible around my desires and utilizing all my energy to maintain that grip, I had finally let it go and was realizing that release was bringing fresh life into my body.

64

I felt like a hot mess who had no idea what was happening in my life. I was on the floor more times than ever before crying out to my Father for His will.

I had never desired it or sought it out in that way.

I had never experienced surrender like that.

And when I finally did, I felt free.

Free from all pressure to work my life out and sort out the problems of everybody else. No longer could I predict what the future held or what His plan was, I was just going with the flow.

Being a hot mess had never felt so good.

And to be honest, I think that is right where our Father wants us, right in this *in-between* – in-between finding total rest in the truth He is good and faithful – then also feeling slightly paralyzed by the reality that we have no control over anything. It is this sweet spot, this treasured space, where you wrestle against your human tendencies of control while doing your best to fully surrender to His ways. It's uncomfortable. It's not easy. But it is certainly the best place to be.

Fighting for surrender.

And I'm not sure we ever really graduate from this place during our time on earth.

Day after day, as new obstacles, emotions, and events come at us, we are forced to continually fight the tendency to grasp for control and instead cling to surrender.

Maybe this is where you are today…a hot mess. Welcome to the club.

YOU DON'T HAVE TO LOOK LIKE
A WARRIOR TO BE ONE.

Here at this club we are learning to acknowledge we don't know it all and we can't do it all. We are finally coming face to face with our shortcomings, and we are trying to accept the truth that we will never be perfect on our own. We are letting go of control and fighting for surrender.

We might be ugly crying with snot running down our faces. We might miss a shower or forget to brush our teeth. Here at the club, we might look like a hot mess and feel like a hot mess, but we are fighting tooth and nail for the beauty and freedom that comes with living a life of surrender.

You don't have to look like a warrior to be one.

RATHER THAN
A PRAYER LIFE DICTATED
BY FEAR, HE DESIRES FOR
US TO ADOPT A PRAYER
LIFE ROOTED IN TRUST.

Take a Minute

Remember

- Your prayers don't need to be anything other than the unedited, unfiltered outpouring of your heart.
- Through continued discipline and experience, through intentional prayer and intentional times of silence, we slowly learn how to hear from the Holy Spirit and discern that voice above the rest.
- The longer we sit on His prompting, the easier it is to talk ourselves out of obedience.
- There is a sweet spot, this treasured space, where you wrestle against your human tendencies of control while doing your best to fully surrender to His ways.
- You don't have to look like a warrior to be one.

Recite

"If you love me, you will keep my commandments. And I will ask the Father, and he will give you another Helper, to be with you forever, even the Spirit of truth, whom the world cannot receive, because it neither sees him nor knows him. You know him, for he dwells with you and will be in you."

John 14:15-17 (ESV)

"Do not merely listen to the word, and so deceive yourselves. Do what it says. Anyone who listens to the word but does not do what it says is like someone who looks at his face in a mirror and, after looking at himself,

69

goes away and immediately forgets what he looks like. But whoever looks intently into the perfect law that gives freedom, and continues in it—not forgetting what they have heard, but doing it—they will be blessed in what they do."

James 1:22-25

"Whoever wants to be my disciple must deny themselves and take up their cross daily and follow me."

Luke 9:23

Reflect

- Have you ever experienced a moment where the Holy Spirit was speaking to you? How did it make you feel?
- Can you think of a moment where the Holy Spirit prompted you and out of fear, you didn't obey? Is there a time He prompted you and you did obey? How were the outcomes different?
- What hard decisions have you had to wrestle through? How did God show up and guide you?
- Have you ever taken a big leap of faith?

Respond

Take a few minutes to talk with God about what is stirring in your heart. Thank Him for the times He has guided you and given you clarity. Repent of the times you have felt prompted by the Holy Spirit, but because of fear, didn't obey. Is there anything in your life you are needing guidance on? Has He already given you the clarity needed, but you haven't been willing to let that be enough. If you are feeling bold, join me in saying this prayer, "Father, where do I need to make changes or move in a different direction?"

Chapter four

for now

for now

I've been alive for 25 years. I've learned a lot, and I also have a lot more learning to do. But if I had to pick one thing I have learned about life so far, here's what I would say: YOU DON'T HAVE CONTROL OVER IT.

And secondly, if life isn't at least a little uncomfortable, that probably means you aren't fully surrendering it to Him.

When I look back at my life, it's a series of me making plans without asking God for His input. Then, God blowing my mind by doing something completely opposite of my plans but so extraordinary I could never have come up with it on my own.

Here is a blurb from something I wrote at the end of June 2018.

> *Two and a half years ago as I prepared to graduate and move home, I was sure I was going to live on my own. As graduation got closer, I decided I would live at home for a year to get settled and enjoy the opportunity to live at home again.*
>
> *A year passed and I still wasn't ready to move out. I loved doing life with my family and was content to be at home. I was saving money and spending time with the people I loved, so I told myself I would give it one more year at home.*
>
> *And here we are at the end of year two, and I still have no desire or plan to move out. This is where I am supposed to be. Having the opportunity to*

spend my days with everyone is a gift I don't take for granted. It is sometimes a hard pill for me to swallow knowing I am the girl still living in my parents' basement, but I wouldn't have it any other way.

Two weeks after writing that, a condo went on the market that I loved. As I was walking through it, I said, "I wish this was on the market six months from now. I'm just not ready to buy."

Four days later I made an offer, and when I was disappointed that I didn't get it, I realized that maybe, just maybe, my Father was trying to tell me something.

I viewed two other properties and didn't get "the feeling," and then a week later a perfect condo went on the market. Showings were starting the day my family and I were leaving for our trip to Yellowstone.

My realtor sent me a video walk-through, and it checked all the boxes. Every. Single. One.

Yet I told my parents, "I would never put an offer on something I hadn't been able to see myself."

The next day my grandparents went to see it for me, and when they called to give their thoughts my grandpa said, "Morgan, I think you would really hate to miss out on this one. It feels like you."

A day later while standing in the middle of Yellowstone National Park surrounded by geysers and bison (seriously), I found one bar of cell phone service and was able to get into my email and sign my offer to buy the condo.

I figured I would leave it all up to Him.

A day later, we managed to find the one place in the whole park that seemed to have some decent cell phone service – a pull-off by a stop sign. As I sat in the car with my family, I listened to the voicemail telling me they had accepted my offer.

As my family cheered, I tried to wrap my mind around what had just happened.

I was a homeowner.

I was moving out.

Subtle panic is probably the closest I can get to describing how I felt. I should have been thrilled, but I was also terrified. What had I just done?

Over the next month I felt like I was drowning. I made more phone calls, sent more emails, and filled out more paperwork than ever before. Half the conversations I had meant nothing to me, and I either had to ask my parents to translate or I had to go back to the person and ask them to try explaining the information to me again.

*Side note: During this whole process I just kept wondering what I had been learning in school for the last 18 years of my life; school is supposed to prepare you for being a grown up right? Well then, why weren't there classes on how to understand a mortgage, apply for a loan, do your taxes, and decide on health insurance. I mean really, my sweet grandparents who live three minutes away have come over at all times of the day to help me with my fire alarm, doorknob, thermostat, and fireplace. All I can say is thank goodness for family who lives nearby and will graciously answer all of my questions (even the ones I should know the answer to).

Anyway, while I was trying to wrap my mind around the logistics of buying a home, I was panicking on the inside wondering what I had done.

Living with my family was good. A month prior to this I was telling friends it just wasn't the right time to buy, and I was content with where I was.

I begged my Father to bring me peace and show me this was truly what He wanted for me. He then reminded me of the prayer I had written at the beginning of 2018.

January 9, 2018

Father, this year I choose the word "bold." While I might already meet the general definition of bold, I believe it means so much more. I want to be bold in seeking You. I want my prayers to be bold. And who knows what might come along this year where You ask me to be bold. I pray when a moment comes where boldness is needed, that I will find my strength in You. May I be bold in Jesus' name.

And that was it. That was all the clarity I needed.

Without me knowing it, He had been preparing my heart for this for a long time.

And come on! Me. Ms. control freak, planner, picky pants, bought her first place without ever having been inside of it. What a joke.

That is when I know it is His will – when something falls so perfectly into place and is so far from what I had planned.

Our Father loves to take our "never" statements and make them come true. He loves to pull the carpet right out from under our feet, because when He does, we have no choice but to grab hold of Him and walk in His plan, His peace, and His grace.

It always brings me back to the verse in Genesis 12 where God tells Abraham, *"Go from your country, your people, and your father's household to the land I will show you. I will make you into a great nation, and I will bless you; I will make your name great, and you will be a blessing."*

This verse was what my Father used to tell me I was supposed to go to school in Tennessee, and now it is the verse that always humbles me in times where I feel uncomfortable and unsure of what He is asking me to do.

Through my years of studying His Word and doing my best to understand the stories of His children and how He has used them for His glory, I have realized the people in the Bible and in the world now, who have made the greatest impact on His Kingdom, have been the ones who were close enough to our Father to hear His voice and then wise enough to be obedient to what He was saying. They trusted His plans without knowing all the details. They simply said yes when He asked them to do something despite the sadness or fear they might have felt.

I think of Moses who got his massive calling from a burning bush and ended up leading God's chosen people out of Egypt. All because he was obedient. Or Rahab who hid the spies. She didn't even realize it was God directing her to do it, but she was still obedient to this little voice inside. Noah was obedient to what seemed like an absurd and ridiculous task, but it was hugely important to the continuation of the world. And then there is Mary. A woman who is dear to all our hearts because her obedience to give birth to and raise our sweet Savior is a piece of the puzzle that saved us all.

So many acts of obedience. Some small and some large, but all incredibly impactful.

And paired with the obedience was faith. The act of saying, "I trust, and I believe despite what I can't see or understand."

"Now faith is confidence in what we hope for and assurance about what we do not see."

Hebrews 11:1

It is faith and obedience that allow us to be vessels for our Father.

Leading up to moving into my new home, there were many days I thought, why did I do this? What is the purpose in having my own space when I was perfectly happy before? Why do I have to live fifteen minutes away from my family?

(And let's be real…years after the move I still think that sometimes. Especially because I'm over there almost every day anyways…yeah, I know. Free dinner and good people, what can I say? I have my priorities straight.)

And every time I come back to the same conclusion – because He told me to.

And that is enough.

Little did I know two years later, I would be saying the same thing as an explanation to people asking, "Why?"

"Why are you leaving teaching?"

"But you were such a good teacher, and those kids need you. Why?"

"Is it because of COVID and what it will look like next year? Is that why you are leaving teaching?"

The questions were endless, and my answer was always the same: "Because God told me to."

I had learned the lesson back in 2013 when my Father told me to go to Tennessee for school and I had learned the lesson in 2018 when He told me it was time to move out.

Obedience ALWAYS wins.

When my Father tells me to do something, whether big or small, I rest in knowing my obedience will be blessed, and He will use me when I am an obedient follower who will trust His plans above my own.

Despite the fear. Despite the trepidation. Despite the sadness. Despite what everyone else said, I was going to be obedient.

He had never let me down before and I knew He never would.

And while I had seen His faithfulness at play so many times in my life and I knew I could trust Him, the human emotions of trepidation, frustration, and uncertainty are all still very real.

And so now 2020 has been added to that list of years my Father told me to do something big.

March 20, 2020

Father, to think that since I last wrote in here nine days ago everything has changed…the whole world is literally shutting down because of COVID…it's wild. Already I am feeling You move in so many ways and I am hearing from You constantly.

79

I have no idea what year it is for you right now as you read this page, but I wonder, what is your reaction when you are reminded of the year 2020?

Do you laugh thinking about how the world fell apart? Do you cry over someone or something you lost in that season? Do you cringe while you reminisce on the memory of being quarantined?

While writing this chapter, I am a little over halfway through 2020 and while I keep thinking there's no way it's going to get worse, I'm pretty sure it will.

This year will go down in the books as one of the craziest. Emotions have run rampant through our world. People are on edge. Relationships are being tested. People are finding their voices.

The world is rising up and it's getting wild.

So, in a season already full of uncertainty, when the middle of March hit, I pretty much had no choice but to throw my hands up in the air like every other human on this planet and say, "Well, who knows what's going to happen. Not sure when I will be let out of my house. Find my sanity. Or put jeans on ever again."

Before I knew it, while I was in the midst of trying to sort through and pray about a massive life shift, everything shut down and I was left with an open schedule, little to do, and WAY too many thoughts to think on.

While I went into those months terrified that I could go crazy without my full schedule and life of adventure, I found a new kind of busy.

My whole calendar was clear and, knowing that would never happen again, I decided to lean in with everything I had to serve His people and grow in His truth.

I filled my days with leading an online book group, leading a prayer gathering, writing this book, learning how to play the guitar, and finally giving myself enough space to read His Word, digest it, and really pray on it.

More than ever before, I was given a glimpse into this idea of ministry, and it felt so right.

Every single day while I sat at home and watched Netflix, went on an endless number of walks, and played a never-ending amount of Wahooie (a Colander family favorite) I always had this question in the back of my mind: "Where am I headed?"

I truly believed ministry was my next step, but with all the changes, that came on a daily basis, I wasn't convinced logistically it would really work out. I started preparing my heart that He might say, "Not yet."

But at the same time, I knew in my gut what He had said at the beginning.

April 20, 2020

Father, here's where I'm at. 10% of me wants to say, "Forget ministry right now. It probably won't work out this year. Just keep waiting." 90% of me says, "You have been preparing my heart for so long. You led me down this road at the beginning of the year for a reason. COVID does not get to come in and ruin Your plans for me. This will be my last year teaching because You are faithful."

April 23, 2020

Father, I don't know the exact plan You have for me, but I know where You have called me. I surrender my plans of this calling to You and say that whatever You ask of me, I will do. Help me to fix my eyes on You.

Day in and day out I sat with the rest of the world wondering what the future held.

I was now five months into this waiting game.

Teaching or ministry?

May 16, 2020

Father, can I be honest? I'm kind of losing my passionate waiting mindset. I am trying so hard to hang onto it…to keep praying about it, to intentionally seek, but at this point I am so confused. I just feel over it. I know You get it and aren't upset. You see my heart in all of this. I trust You and I want Your will, but it's getting frustrating. I have no idea where You want me at this point. I figure if the church says yes then I will go there, and if not, I teach. I just want to seek Your will with a pure heart and not with frustration. I think I'll feel frustrated if it's not the church because what a confusing journey…but I prayed for Your will, not mine.

A few days later the church reached out to set up a time to talk.

May 20, 2020

Okay God, here I am. Holding out my plans in suspension. You will either open the door of ministry and I will walk through it, or You close it right now and tell me to stay in teaching. Your will, not mine…

May 21, 2020

Father, the church wants me. You opened the door, and I am going to walk through it. I don't know all the details, but this is where You want me. You are so faithful. Your love for me and plan for my life astounds me. Surrender…I think You have finally given me my word for 2020. Here I thought I had my life mapped out and You have changed everything.

And just like that, I had made my decision (or so I thought). I thought the struggle was over, the peace would flow freely, and my heart would calm down.

But, I am learning life doesn't normally work that way.

I tried to make it easy on myself – if the church wanted me, that was my signal from God to go for it.

But that idea sounded easier than it actually was.

What I found was there were two different kinds of surrender. One was the desire to surrender – *aspiring surrender* – and the other was the actual act of surrender – *active surrender.*

Over the last few months, I wrestled to adopt this idea of surrender. I fought to let go of my plans and my control, and in doing so, I really began to ask my Father where He wanted me. At first, it was incredibly unnatural. While I thought I was living according to His will, I learned I was better at planning the course and then running it by Him after I had acted on it, rather than asking Him to map it all out for me.

I learned what it looked like to seek His will and not mine. I learned what it felt like to live in suspension simply waiting for Him to guide each step.

While I had not mastered this, I had come a long way the last few months. I was emotionally and spiritually ready and willing to give up complete control, but all of a sudden being willing to give up control and actually follow through with it was two separate fights.

I was all in when it came to *aspiring surrender* but hadn't quite found my footing with *active surrender.*

June 10, 2020

Father, I feel so lost. I feel confused and worn out. Literally exhausted from trying to figure out your plan for me. What if this job isn't right for me?

June 11, 2020

Father, control my mind please. Fill me with life, peace, and guidance. You are my strength and my song. You alone can redeem my every thought. Make clear my next step. That is as far as I need to see.

"Make clear my next step." Not my next five steps, ten steps, or next mile.

"Your own ears will hear him. Right behind you a voice will say, 'This is the way you should go,' whether to the right or to the left."

Isaiah 30:21(NLT)

"We can make our plans, but the LORD determines our steps."

Proverbs 16:9 (NLT)

Because I'm a planner, this is a tough pill to swallow. So many different times the Bible tells us our Father will guide us. He will make clear the path before us.

But the Bible never promises He will reveal the whole path to us. That He will show us the destination before we begin our trek.

It just tells us He will guide us as we go.

• • •

One of my favorite things in this whole world – aside from Jesus, my family, friends, and donuts – is summiting Colorado 14ers.

I'll spare you my enormous passion-filled soap box speech about how immaculate and magnificent they are and instead just help you imagine one piece of it.

As most everyone knows, Colorado weather is highly unpredictable. We can go from sunshine, to rain, to snow, and back to sunshine in a matter of an hour. While this can annoy some people, personally I think it adds to the adventure of life and it keeps us humans a little more flexible. That's the enneagram 7 in me…always wanting more adventure and more fun.

Anyway, at an elevation of 14,000 feet, you often run into afternoon storms, which can be detrimental. Your goal, and plan, is to get up and down as fast as you can before you catch yourself hustling down a slippery slope and seeking shelter. The best way to do this is to get an early start, and best early starts are in the dark.

When you start before sunrise, your path is illuminated about five feet in front of you with your headlamp, so aside from those five feet, you can't see anything else. You simply follow the guiding light one step at a time trusting it is the way you need to go.

While it has a different and a bit of an uncomfortable feel to it, I always say my time spent climbing in the dark is so sweet because I don't have the chance to get worked up about what's coming next. If there is a massive hill to climb, I can't see how long it goes for or how big it is. Instead, I just take one step at a time slowly gaining mileage and elevation.

Most of the time, whether I'm summiting a 14er or just making my way through life, I have found that seeing too much of the journey at once can be debilitating.

There is one reason our Father doesn't reveal our whole life to us at once.

He knows we can't handle it.

If we knew the trials, challenges, obstacles, and tough times we were going to encounter in life, we would panic and find ourselves full of fear or potentially even change courses to try and keep ourselves from those experiences.

Naturally, we want to take the easiest, most painless route.

But if we do that, the destination is disappointing.

We might find ourselves in the wrong relationship because staying in it seemed easier than ending it.

We might find ourselves in a career we have no passion for because fear stopped us from pursuing our calling.

We might find ourselves lonely and isolated because we aren't willing to give the effort that is required to find community and close-knit friendships.

The easy route doesn't equal the fruitful route.

Life is better lived in the dark where you can see what's right in front of you and nothing more.

A five-foot radius around us is about all we need.

Looking back, we can see some of our past, on either side we have access to those closest to us, and in front of us we see the next step we have to take.

Anything more and we would flounder.

We may not know our destination, what trials are coming our way, or exactly what our route is going to look like, but we can trust the light guiding us.

"Your word is a lamp to guide my feet and a light for my path."

Psalm 119:105 (NLT)

When we ask Him, He will always show us the next step.

I prayed for a heart of surrender and my Father has given me that. I prayed for open doors and my Father has also given me that. He has given me all I needed to make my final decision, but pulling the trigger was proving to be tougher than I had anticipated.

As I said earlier, the desire for surrender is different than the act of surrender.

I could talk the talk well. For the last five months I had been telling God I was willing to surrender it all to Him. I told Him I would go where He called me. I told Him as long as He showed me the way I would follow.

But all of a sudden, He had shown me the way and following it wasn't easy.

I could *talk* all day about surrendering, but now I was *having* to surrender.

Teaching or ministry? Teaching or ministry? Teaching or ministry?

That was all my brain could focus on. I could not make the final call.

I was driving in the car and said, "God, I thought I was called to be a teacher and now I'm feeling called to ministry. What do you want me to do?"

My Father gently whispered something that changed my life forever.

He said, "I have not called you to be a teacher. I have not called you to ministry. I have called you to minister."

To minister anywhere and everywhere. In any and every way.

A friend reminded me recently that often as humans we seek to live in a world of absolutes.

We make claims about buying a house that we will live in forever. We say we will never leave our job or move to another state. We promise to never get a divorce or say we will never have kids. We tell our parents we will never move them into a nursing home.

I grew up believing I was going to be a teacher and never gave space to the idea it would only be for four years.

We find comfort in the control absolutes bring to our lives. They make us feel like we know what is coming and like we have the power to make all those decisions and plans.

But our God is not a God of our absolutes.

"Therefore do not worry about tomorrow, for tomorrow will worry about itself. Each day has enough trouble of its own."

Matthew 6:34

Our Father very clearly tells us we are to live for today. Trying to live in a world of our own absolutes only exhausts us as we try to take the burden of control upon ourselves when He has already promised us, He will carry the weight of that. He will do the heavy lifting and the hard thinking about what is coming in the following days, months, and years. We are just to walk with Him one day at a time.

So while He isn't a God of our absolutes, He is a God of "for now's."

> For now you are taking a break from getting your degree.
> For now you can't have children.
> For now you need to take care of your parents.
> For now this is where you need to serve.
> For now this is where you are going to live.
> For now you are single.
> For now you are a teacher.

Let me be clear about one thing – nothing is forever except Him.

The only thing we can count on, as a constant in our life, is our Father. Everything else is shifting. Everything else is a "for now."

———

SO WHILE HE ISN'T A GOD OF ABSOLUTES, HE IS A GOD OF "FOR NOWS."

———

I believed teaching was my absolute. I imagined retiring when I became a mom, but never thought I would step away from my dream job to change careers.

So, while I was sitting in my car begging my Father for an absolute – teaching or ministry – He gently told me my career isn't an absolute, but my calling is.

For a while I was a teacher.

For now I am in ministry.

Forever I am to minister.

I don't know where you are right now. Maybe you feel like you are stuck in an absolute that makes you utterly miserable and you see no way out. Maybe, like me, you are giving up something you thought was an absolute you really loved. Maybe you like the idea of an absolute because it feels like there is nothing sure and steady in your life.

———

NOTHING IS FOREVER
EXCEPT HIM.

———

Wherever you are, I feel you. I resonate with you. I get it.

The idea of living in a world of absolutes sounds reassuring and feels comforting. It feels good to make forever decisions about your life, so you have an idea of where you are going and what is to come. In a world that seems to always be in chaos, it makes you feel in control of something.

But, as I am learning right alongside you, living in a world of absolutes only does one thing to us – limits us from fully surrendering and living into the purpose and plan our Father has for us.

His plan for you is so much greater than a few absolutes.

His plan for you includes a million and one "for now's" that in the end will add up to a beautiful, perfectly crafted, fulfilling life of serving Him and loving His people.

And nothing is better than that.

So, while it still stings a little bit to say...for a while I was a teacher and for now that season is over. For now, I am in ministry working at my church.

As soon as this truth became clear to me, that I was to minister, I felt at peace giving up the title "teacher."

I knew my Father was asking me to step out of that career and step into a new one.

While I was tempted to continue to weigh the pros and cons of my decision, ask God for more clarity, and sit on the decision a while longer, I knew what He was asking me to do.

Let's be real, I knew what He wanted me to do five months before.

Now it was time to act on it.

July 7, 2020

Father, today is my first day at the church. As I try to wrap my mind around it all, I pray You would use me. Your will be done. Father, I am doing this literally because You told me to. I pray I will do my best and that my efforts will be fruitful. Father, I want to be a part of Your Kingdom building. May I reflect You...thank You for choosing me.

OBEDIENCE
ALWAYS
WINS.

Take a Minute

Remember

- It is faith and obedience that allow us to be vessels for our Father.
- Obedience ALWAYS wins.
- Aspiring surrender isn't the same as active surrender.
- The easy route doesn't equal the fruitful route.
- So while He isn't a God of our absolutes, He is a God of "for nows."
- Nothing is forever except Him.
- His plan for you includes a million and one "for now's" that in the end will add up to a beautiful, perfectly crafted, fulfilling life of serving Him and loving His people.

Recite

"Go from your country, your people, and your father's household to the land I will show you. I will make you into a great nation, and I will bless you; I will make your name great, and you will be a blessing."

Genesis 12:1-2

"Now faith is confidence in what we hope for and assurance about what we do not see."

Hebrews 11:1

"Your own ears will hear him. Right behind you a voice will say, 'This is the way you should go,' whether to the right or to the left."

Isaiah 30:21 (NLT)

"We can make our plans, but the LORD determines our steps."

Proverbs 16:9 (NLT)

"Your word is a lamp to guide my feet and a light for my path."

Psalm 119:105 (NLT)

"Therefore do not worry about tomorrow, for tomorrow will worry about itself. Each day has enough trouble of its own."

Matthew 6:34

Reflect

- Has God ever called you to walk away from something or someone you loved? Maybe it was something you were really good at. Was it hard to do? Have you seen the fruit of your obedience?
- Looking back at your life, can you see why God doesn't reveal His whole plan to us?
- Is there an easy route you have taken that has led to disappointment?
- God has called you to minister. What does that mean to you?
- What "absolutes" do you need to let go of and replace with "for now's"?

Respond

Take a few minutes to talk with God about what is stirring in your heart. Thank Him for being bigger than your "never statements" and writing a story for you that is perfect. Ask Him if there is an easy path you have taken you need to stop walking on. Ask Him how you can minister right where you are. And finally, thank Him for protecting your heart by only giving you one step at a time. Then ask, "What's my next step?"

Chapter five

step out of the boat

step out of the boat

August 21, 2020

Can I be honest?

Can I level with you where I'm at right now?

Everyone tells me I'm lucky to have left the classroom and then they tell me I will be great anywhere I go.

Right now, I completely disagree.

In the last few months my world has flipped upside down, and so far, it hasn't flipped right side up again.

I feel like I'm in a permanent handstand doing everything I can to keep from crashing to the ground. I'm trying to stay upright, but the longer I go, the more my head throbs, the more fatigued I become, and the dizzier I get.

I am stuck upside down and I'm not sure when I will feel right side up.

The worst part of it is I didn't anticipate feeling this way. I thought the peace my Father gave me in taking this step would overpower and dissolve all the other emotions and thoughts. Well, it hasn't.

I want to stand tall and say I feel great. That I feel settled. That I feel content.

But I don't.

I feel incapable. I feel insecure. I feel anxious. I feel left out. I feel uncertain.

I feel like this is turning out to be a lot harder than I thought it would be.

I felt called my whole life to be a teacher. I pretended I was a teacher up until the point I could train to be one. Then I studied and practiced until finally I had a diploma and a job.

I remember my first day of teaching. I remember standing there with 22 kids sitting on the rug anxiously waiting for me to give them direction. To lead and guide and grow and love them for the next nine months. I remember this mix of excitement and fear making my heart beat fast. I had done it. My dream had come true. This was it.

Every day after for the next four years I was in my happy place. Sure, there were days when I wanted to pull my hair out and days when I thought a cubicle where I had a minute of peace sounded appealing, but in the end, nothing was better than my classroom. It was my second home and I felt more myself in there than I did almost anywhere else.

I never worried I wasn't good at it. Yes, I had lots of learning to do and would never reach the point where I had mastered the art of teaching, but I knew I was good at my job. The kids loved me, parents loved me, and each day I saw my kids progressing.

Like any job, there were things I wasn't good at. Students that didn't grow as much as I would have hoped. Parents who weren't always happy with me. Deadlines I missed. Days I messed up.

But I was proud of what I did. And I knew I was making a difference.

With each hug from a kid, kind email from a parent, or increased test score, I gained confidence knowing what I was doing was working. My kids were growing in academic knowledge but also growing in their ability to empathize with others and be kind.

I left each day feeling accomplished even if the day had been a train wreck. I knew we had tomorrow to start over, start fresh, and keep learning.

When people asked me what I did, I was always so proud to tell them I was a teacher. It was my pride and joy to carry around that title. It had been my dream.

And now it's gone.

I was a teacher, but I'm not one anymore, and that hurts.

When people ask me what I do, answering that question stings a little.

I want to tell them I used to be a teacher, because letting that part of me go is killing me.

It's like losing a part of myself.

Without that title, I'm feeling a little lost, which scares me even more.

Until that title was taken from me, I didn't realize how much of my identity was tied up in it. I hadn't recognized how much pride came from it. I didn't know how much self-worth I got from it.

Hanging upside down, I'm coming face to face with some truths I hadn't ever known, and they hurt.

I don't believe my Father asked me to leave teaching because He solely wanted me to realize these truths, but I do believe He knew these truths were going to be something I would wrestle with in leaving teaching.

He knew I was prideful. He knew my self-worth was tied up in a career. He knew my identity was fueled by teaching.

It was me who had no idea about these things, and now I have to sort them out.

Since the big switch, it seems like every day I find myself deeper and deeper in a pit because with each day comes more heartbreak and realization of what teaching was to me, and how I will have to work on my heart to heal the hole that is now there. I know eventually I will start making my way out of the pit and will find myself standing on top. It just may not be right away, and that is okay.

While I feel like these feelings are so not me, I'm going to let myself sit in the feelings and sort and pray through them one day at a time.

Here's what I'm learning – His peace doesn't supersede your feelings.

I feel an overwhelming peace that I'm where I need to be, but that doesn't negate everything else I'm feeling.

I thought being filled with His peace meant I wouldn't feel things like anxiety, insecurity, and doubt, but that isn't the case.

Being filled with His peace means you have the power to pray through, process through, and conquer those other feelings in time. It means while you may feel them, they won't take over. They will not define you. They will not be victorious.

———

HIS PEACE DOESN'T
SUPERSEDE YOUR FEELINGS.

———

His peace allows us the chance to fight those feelings with the power of His grace through wrestling and prayer and patience.

Being obedient and walking in His will, doesn't guarantee happiness all the time. It guarantees eternal joy.

You can be in His will and be full of His peace, yet still feel insecure, anxious, and unsure.

The difference is those emotions are fleeting and His peace is everlasting.

I'm at a good place—physically and emotionally and spiritually.

Working at the church is such a gift. I always wanted to be a part of it all, and here I am.

Being surrounded by people who are so determined to preach the Gospel and help the lost find their way home is remarkable.

I have no doubt this is where He wants me.

And when it comes to all my internal struggles, I know they are refining me.

While I wasn't intentionally finding my self-worth in teaching, I know it's time I found all of my self-worth in Him.

I didn't mean to be so prideful, but it's about time I was knocked down from my pedestal and bowed down to the only One who deserves praise.

And my identity should never be found in anything other than in being the daughter of the King.

I don't like the reality of sorting through all of this, praying through it, and coming to terms with where my heart is at, but this is exactly where I need to be.

Growing in Him. Being refined, renewed, and built up.

I feel incapable, insecure, anxious, left out, and uncertain, but I am filled to the brim with His peace. That alone is enough. His joy is my strength. His presence is all I need.

Obedience doesn't equate to seamless and easy, but it always leads to fulfillment and fullness of joy.

• • •

Here I am four weeks out from what you just read feeling more off kilter than ever, but at the same time feeling more grounded than ever.

I don't really know how to explain it.

OBEDIENCE DOESN'T EQUATE
TO SEAMLESS AND EASY, BUT IT ALWAYS LEADS
TO FULFILLMENT AND FULLNESS OF JOY.

Faith is a funny thing in that way – it doesn't always make sense. It doesn't always line up. It isn't always logical (which is really hard for me).

It's more of a feeling. This deep gut feeling of being settled rather than unsettled. Feeling content rather than anxious. Feeling peace rather than uneasiness. Even in the midst of a mess.

I feel like the disciple Peter right now, walking on water aiming to inch closer and closer to Jesus.

This passage of Scripture shows us a perfect example of what happens when we choose to surrender and step out in faith.

Shortly before dawn Jesus went out to them, walking on the lake.

When the disciples saw him walking on the lake, they were terrified. "It's a ghost," they said, and cried out in fear.

But Jesus immediately said to them: "Take courage! It is I. Don't be afraid."

"Lord, if it's you," Peter replied, "tell me to come to you on the water."

"Come," he said.

Then Peter got down out of the boat, walked on the water and came toward Jesus.

But when he saw the wind, he was afraid and, beginning to sink, cried out, "Lord, save me!"

Immediately, Jesus reached out his hand and caught him. "You of little faith," he said, "why did you doubt?"

And when they climbed into the boat, the wind died down. Then those who were in the boat worshiped him, saying, "Truly you are the Son of God."

Matthew 14:25-33

Peter desired to live a life of faith. He wanted to act out of faith and do something that was going to bring him closer to Jesus, and so Peter asked Jesus for an opportunity. He asked Jesus to call him out on the water.

"I have been crucified with Christ. It is no longer I who live, but Christ who lives in me. And the life I now live in the flesh I live by faith in the Son of God, who loved me and gave himself for me."

Galatians 2:20 (ESV)

Our Father wants us to live a life motivated by our firm relentless trust in who He is. More than anything He desires that our faith be the guiding light for everything, but He won't force that upon us. Instead, He eagerly awaits the moment we reach out to Him desiring to live that life of faith rather than living by our flesh.

In wanting to grow his faith and come nearer to Jesus, Peter asks Jesus to call him out onto the water.

Have you ever asked Jesus to call you out onto the water?

For me, I think back to 2019 and all those prayers of anticipation. I felt my Father working in me, I was feeling a shift in my heart for something more, and eventually it brought me to a place of total surrender. I finally realized the life I had been living was one I had every intention of using to glorify Him, but I was lacking the piece that made building His Kingdom so fruitful – surrender.

I asked God one itty bitty question. "Where do I need to make changes or move in a different direction?" He came in and wrecked my world.

You see, in wanting to come nearer to Him, I asked Him to give me the opportunity.

And He wasted no time.

I don't believe our Father is one who pushes growth down our throat. If we want to stay stagnant, He will sit with us. But the minute we desire to grow, He jumps at the opportunity to teach us, mold us, and refine us.

Jesus didn't demand Peter come walk on the water. No, Peter asked to be invited.

Peter asked Jesus for the chance to challenge and grow his faith.

He asked for the opportunity to surrender and trust.

And because Jesus desires for us to come near to Him, to act on our faith, to trust, He told Peter, "Come."

He said the same to me, and He says the same to you.

As soon as I asked for the chance to grow, He gave it to me.

As soon as you ask Him how you can act on your faith and draw nearer to Him, He will tell you.

He's eagerly waiting for you to ask.

Peter took action.

With a boldness that only comes from deep-seeded trust, Peter stepped out of the boat onto water and began walking towards Jesus.

I think all too often we ask God for the chance to be bold, to act on our faith, to grow, and then when He provides us with the opportunity, we do nothing.

Again, *aspiring surrender* is different than *active surrender*.

It is easy to ask God to show us where to go. To be open to the idea of making changes in our life. To desire the boldness to make sacrifices for His glory. But none of that is the same as actually acting on His leading.

When Jesus told Peter to come, Peter didn't waiver, weigh the pros and cons, and then say, "Actually, never-mind Jesus. The water is pretty deep, it's kind of chilly, and I don't really feel like stepping out in faith to potentially drown. I think I'm good here. Thanks for the invite though."

No, Peter stepped out on the water and while he might have done it with no hesitation, to make myself feel better, I would like to imagine this – that after Jesus extended the invitation Peter stood on the edge of the boat weighing the pros and cons, dipping his toes in only to realize how cold the water was and pull his foot back up into the boat, to just dip the other toe in, all while saying to himself over and over, "Come on Peter you can do this. Don't be such a chicken. He's got me." And then finally after convincing himself to go on the count of three – one…two…three – he went for it.

I would also like to imagine Peter thought all the same things I did: "This is crazy. What am I thinking? Well, here goes nothing. No turning back now. What do I have to lose other than everything? I hope I made the right choice…Wait, I take it back…No, never-mind, it's okay, I've got this. He's never let me down before, and I know He won't start now."

Peter went for it. He stepped out of the boat.

Is God asking you to step out of the boat?

Is there an opportunity you have been dipping your toes in but are lacking the courage to go for it?

Well, hey, welcome to the club.

Peter, me, and a whole lot of other followers of Jesus feel you and know exactly what you are going through.

It's scary, isn't it?

Day in and day out you run through all the things that could go wrong if you go for it. You think of every worst-case scenario. You ponder all the ways it could blow up in your face.

Yep, I know it all too well.

Let me give you a little tip...go for it.

If He is calling you, don't hesitate. Don't question. Don't overthink. Go for it.

Step out of the boat.

"...for we walk by faith, not by sight."

2 Corinthians 5:7 (ESV)

You probably can't see how it will all turn out. Chances are you can't even see what's beyond the next turn. That's okay, take the one step you can see.

Just step out of the boat.

After stepping out of the boat, Peter does what we all would do, he loses focus. I mean, come on, he is standing *on top of* water so I imagine the thoughts running through his head are something like, "Woah, this is wild. I can't believe I am actually walking on water."

Then, he takes his focus off Jesus. He looks to the left, to the right, and I'm sure he looked down over and over to see if his feet were truly on top of the water. In a split second, after the excitement dissipates, he begins to become more aware of his surroundings. No longer focused on Jesus standing in front of him, guiding him one step at a time, he sees the wind and loses his stability. He begins to feel fear and then it happens…he begins to sink.

The minute he took the leap of faith, Peter got distracted, listened to sounds other than the voice of Jesus, and began to sink.

Yep, that's me. Guilty as charged.

For whatever reason, I assumed as soon as I made my decision official – sent in my resignation letter and signed the acceptance letter – I would be good to go.

I figured that in being obedient and following His leading, everything to follow would be swell and smooth sailing.

I didn't take my eyes off of Jesus, per se, but I absolutely was not prepared for the battle that awaited me on the other side of the decision. I was not prepared for the other voices that would clamor for my attention.

Voices that told me I should be insecure, question who I am, and wonder if I am actually any good at this job.

Voices that told me I needed the praise of the people to feel valued and loved.

Voices that made me wonder what in the world I was thinking.

I listened to these voices instead of solely listening to His strong, sure, steady voice that kept saying, "One step at a time, Morgan. Focus on Me and don't worry about anything else. I've got you."

I made space for the enemy to attack, unaware of the vulnerable place I was at, and because of that I began to sink.

Maybe you feel that right now. You know Jesus is standing right in front of you, assuring you each step of the way, but rather than focusing on His voice, you have made space for other voices. For lies to creep in. For the enemy to plant seeds of fear, doubt, and insecurity in your life.

Maybe you are beginning to sink.

I don't know, maybe you are already sunk. Fully immersed and stuck at the bottom.

Either way, I have good news for you.

He'll catch you.

After beginning to sink, Peter cries out to Jesus to save him, and the Bible tells us Jesus **immediately** reached out his hand to Peter and caught him from sinking.

Without hesitation. Without a lecture. Without a shake of the finger.

With just one cry for help, Jesus reached out and caught him.

He pulled Peter out of the water and steadied him.

I can imagine the relief Peter must have felt. One minute he is walking on water. The next minute he's sinking. And then in an instant, Jesus is pulling him up out of the water.

Just take a minute and imagine the Son of God pulling you up out of the water. In a state of sheer panic, fearful you are going to drown, you are lifted up and made safe. I imagine the touch of Jesus flooding Peter with feelings of security and peace.

Because that's what our Father is for us. Safety. Security. A refuge. A place of comfort. A place of peace. A place rid of fear and doubt.

With a simple cry, He will catch us.

I wanted to be strong enough to do it on my own. I had no desire to admit my heart and insides were all jumbled up in a big mess of fear, doubt, and confusion.

When people (literally everyone) asked me, "How is the new job? Do you miss teaching?" I wanted to be able to honestly and with a joyful spunk say, "It is a dream come true. I loved teaching, but I don't miss it at all. It has all been perfect."

I wanted it to be seamless, easy, and graceful.

But it wasn't and until I was willing to admit that and cry out to my Father, I was going to sink further and further.

My pride. My shame. My disappointment.

They were all standing in the way – keeping me from crying out to my Father who only wanted to scoop me up out of the water and hold me in His arms while I cried to Him and told Him how hard this really was. How sad I was to be done teaching. How scared I was to be in a job that made me feel less secure. How much I desperately needed Him to pull through on this for me because He is the only reason I was in this mess.

And finally, when I cried out, when I was willing to recognize what was truly going on, the walls broke down, and the peace and comfort of my Father flooded in.

I have found that trying to prove my strength on my own only generates one feeling – exhaustion. It leaves me feeling weary from putting a smile on my face while ignoring all the other emotions I'm feeling. I find myself constantly giving pep talks in my head as I try to convince myself I am fine and need to just keep moving forward. Essentially, I end up faking it, to myself and others, that all is well, and it drains my soul. It sucks the life out of me.

I imagine Peter as he began to sink, and it is the same image I have of myself before admitting to where I was. Sinking under the weight of it all, too exhausted to try and fight it.

Have you ever felt this way?

Doing life on your own, carrying the burden and weight of all your decisions and those of the people around you, is terrible.

Let's be honest…doing life without our Savior is the worst.

But doing life with Him, oh man, it's the sweetest.

I've got a feeling that in one way or another you are sinking. Whether it be in one specific area or just life in general, each day you are getting deeper and deeper, feeling the weight of that exhaustion.

It doesn't have to be that way.

Just like Jesus was with Peter, He is right there waiting for you to cry out to Him.

In Matthew 11, our Father reminds us He offers us a burden that is light and in Him we can find rest.

Rest in the midst of confusion, fear, or the greatest turmoil. No matter the situation, no matter the emotions, He will lift you up and give you rest. You just have to take hold of it.

"Take my yoke upon you and learn from me, for I am gentle and humble in heart, and you will find rest for your souls. For my yoke is easy and my burden is light."

Matthew 11:29-30

Cry out to Him and *immediately* He will reach out His hand and catch you.

The freedom I felt from finally recognizing and admitting how I felt and how much I desperately needed His continued presence in my life was the greatest feeling ever.

It didn't take away all the doubts, uncertainties, or fears, but in giving those feelings over to Him, I was able to experience a lightness in my step and a feeling of sweet, unburdened rest.

I've learned that we must keep our eyes fixed on Jesus. He is the only steady and sure person in this world.

"Let us fix our eyes on Jesus, the author and perfector of our faith…"

Hebrews 12:2 (BSB)

So go ahead, step out of the boat and when you do, keep looking right at Him.

Spend time in the Word, write down your prayers, keep a gratitude journal, find a community of other followers of Jesus to do life with, plug into a church, praise Him with a song…do whatever it takes to stay in a growing relationship with Him.

I hit the bottom of my pit when I recognized I couldn't do this life on my own. And now, I'm climbing my way out of the pit with His help. Sure, my Father could just lift me right out of the pit, but He knows better than that, and so do I.

As I slowly climb upward, I'm wrestling through and exposing the lies I have believed, the false sense of security I had in my career, and every day finding more and more power, strength, and identity in who my Father says I am.

Rather than an immediate healing, I need this time to process, reflect, and grow. I need to be refined to look more like my Father. I need to surrender it all at His feet each and every day.

Psalms 40 captures this so beautifully. David has clearly just been delivered from some sort of difficult circumstance. He begins by praising God for His faithfulness in lifting him out of the pit. He goes on to write about the redemptive work of Jesus and then recognizes the forgiveness of our Father and the desperate need we all have for Him.

I waited patiently for the Lord;
he turned to me and heard my cry.
He lifted me out of the slimy pit,
out of the mud and mire;
he set my feet on a rock

115

and gave me a firm place to stand.
He put a new song in my mouth,
a hymn of praise to our God.
Many will see and fear the Lord
and put their trust in him.

Blessed is the one
who trusts in the Lord,
who does not look to the proud,
to those who turn aside to false gods.
Many, Lord my God,
are the wonders you have done,
the things you planned for us.
None can compare with you;
were I to speak and tell of your deeds,
they would be too many to declare.

Sacrifice and offering you did not desire—
but my ears you have opened—
burnt offerings and sin offerings you did not require.
Then I said, "Here I am, I have come—
it is written about me in the scroll.
I desire to do your will, my God;
your law is within my heart."

I proclaim your saving acts in the great assembly;
I do not seal my lips, Lord,
as you know.
I do not hide your righteousness in my heart;
I speak of your faithfulness and your saving help.
I do not conceal your love and your faithfulness
from the great assembly.

Do not withhold your mercy from me, Lord;
may your love and faithfulness always protect me.
For troubles without number surround me;
my sins have overtaken me, and I cannot see.
They are more than the hairs of my head,
and my heart fails within me.
Be pleased to save me, Lord;
come quickly, Lord, to help me.

May all who want to take my life
be put to shame and confusion;
may all who desire my ruin
be turned back in disgrace.
May those who say to me, "Aha! Aha!"
be appalled at their own shame.
But may all who seek you
rejoice and be glad in you;
may those who long for your saving help always say,
"The Lord is great!"

But as for me, I am poor and needy;
may the Lord think of me.
You are my help and my deliverer;
you are my God, do not delay.

Psalm 40

Take a minute and let that Psalm sink into your heart.

What parts of that Psalm struck a chord with you?

117

Meditate on the ways your Father has already lifted you out of the pit and praise Him for His goodness to you.

Rest in the truth that we are all in need of Him.

He is our deliverer. When we cry out to Him, He hears us and will catch us.

•••

Let's circle back around to Peter's story once more to point out my favorite and most relatable part of the story.

Right after Jesus reaches out to catch Peter, Jesus says to him, "You of little faith. Why do you doubt?"

Now listen closely. Up until this point Peter had witnessed Jesus heal the blind, sick, demon-possessed, and paralyzed. Just earlier that day Jesus had fed 5,000 men, plus all the women and children, with five loaves of bread and two fish.

Peter had clearly witnessed and experienced the miracles of Jesus and had seen He was capable of anything, yet he still doubted.

And Jesus calls him out on it.

"Peter, come on man. You've seen what I can do. Why can't you just have the faith to trust Me fully and believe that I will always come through for you. That I will never let you down."

Yowza. I've heard that way too many times from my Father.

In His most loving voice I hear Him saying, *"Morgan, come on. We've been through this, and you do this every time I ask you to trust Me. I've never let you down before and I'm not ever going to. How many more times do I need to prove this to you? I've got you."*

He's right. I have no reason to doubt His faithfulness, yet just about every time He asks me to step out of the boat, I question His abilities and His direction.

"Are you sure, God? Do you promise You will take care of me?"

You would think by now, with more than 25 years behind me of insane faithfulness from Him, I would quit the questions and doubts. But they still linger.

And when I start to question His guidance and where He's taking me, I feel Him saying to me what He said to Peter, "Come on, stop doubting Me. You know I will take care of it all."

Human nature at its finest.

Doubting and questioning the most stable, loving, and consistent person in our life.

Do you feel me on this? Are you guilty of this constant cycle of doubting Him, being reminded of His goodness, trusting Him, and then going back to doubting?

If not, teach me your ways.

But if you are, then again, welcome to the club.

In our attempts to live a life of surrender, may we continue to grow in our trust, ditch the doubting, and have faith beyond what we can imagine.

Until then, thank goodness for our Father's unlimited patience and willingness to scoop us up when we begin to sink.

WE MUST KEEP OUR EYES
FIXED ON JESUS. HE IS THE
ONLY STEADY AND SURE
PERSON IN THIS WORLD.

Take a Minute

Remember

- His peace doesn't supersede your feelings. Being filled with His peace means you have the power to pray through, process through, and conquer those other feelings in time. It means while you may feel them, they won't take over. They will not define you. They will not be victorious.
- Obedience doesn't equate to seamless and easy, but it always leads to fulfillment and fullness of joy.
- Faith is this deep gut feeling of being settled rather than unsettled. Feeling content rather than anxious. Feeling peace rather than uneasiness. Even in the midst of a mess.
- Our Father wants us to live a life motivated by our firm relentless trust in who He is.
- Step out of the boat.
- With a simple cry, He will catch us.
- We must keep our eyes fixed on Jesus. He is the only steady and sure person in this world.

Recite

Shortly before dawn Jesus went out to them, walking on the lake.

When the disciples saw him walking on the lake, they were terrified. "It's a ghost," they said, and cried out in fear.

But Jesus immediately said to them: "Take courage! It is I. Don't be afraid."

123

"Lord, if it's you," Peter replied, *"tell me to come to you on the water."*

"Come," he said.

Then Peter got down out of the boat, walked on the water and came toward Jesus.

But when he saw the wind, he was afraid and, beginning to sink, cried out, "Lord, save me!"

Immediately, Jesus reached out his hand and caught him. "You of little faith," he said, "why did you doubt?"

And when they climbed into the boat, the wind died down. Then those who were in the boat worshiped him, saying, "Truly you are the Son of God."

Matthew 14:25-33

"I have been crucified with Christ. It is no longer I who live, but Christ who lives in me. And the life I now live in the flesh I live by faith in the Son of God, who loved me and gave himself for me."

Galatians 2:20 (ESV)

"For we walk by faith, not by sight."

2 Corinthians 5:7 (ESV)

"Take my yoke upon you and learn from me, for I am gentle and humble in heart, and you will find rest for your souls. For my yoke is easy and my burden is light."

Matthew 11:29-30

"Let us fix our eyes on Jesus, the author and perfecter of our faith..."

Hebrews 12:2 (BSB)

I waited patiently for the Lord;
he turned to me and heard my cry.
He lifted me out of the slimy pit,
out of the mud and mire;
he set my feet on a rock
and gave me a firm place to stand.
He put a new song in my mouth,
a hymn of praise to our God.
Many will see and fear the Lord
and put their trust in him.

Blessed is the one
who trusts in the Lord,
who does not look to the proud,
to those who turn aside to false gods.
Many, Lord my God,
are the wonders you have done,
the things you planned for us.
None can compare with you;
were I to speak and tell of your deeds,
they would be too many to declare.

Sacrifice and offering you did not desire—
but my ears you have opened—
burnt offerings and sin offerings you did not require.
Then I said, "Here I am, I have come—
it is written about me in the scroll.
I desire to do your will, my God;
your law is within my heart."

I proclaim your saving acts in the great assembly;
I do not seal my lips, Lord,
as you know.
I do not hide your righteousness in my heart;
I speak of your faithfulness and your saving help.
I do not conceal your love and your faithfulness
from the great assembly.

Do not withhold your mercy from me, Lord;
may your love and faithfulness always protect me.
For troubles without number surround me;
my sins have overtaken me, and I cannot see.
They are more than the hairs of my head,
and my heart fails within me.
Be pleased to save me, Lord;
come quickly, Lord, to help me.

May all who want to take my life
be put to shame and confusion;
may all who desire my ruin
be turned back in disgrace.
May those who say to me, "Aha! Aha!"
be appalled at their own shame.
But may all who seek you
rejoice and be glad in you;
may those who long for your saving help always say,
"The Lord is great!"

But as for me, I am poor and needy;
may the Lord think of me.
You are my help and my deliverer;
you are my God, do not delay.

Psalm 40

Reflect

- Have you ever asked God to call you out onto the water? If you did, was your request followed up with action?
- Where in Peter's story can you relate most right now? Is God asking you to step out of the boat? Are you beginning to sink? Have you already sunk? If so, what is keeping you from crying out to your Father, asking Him to come scoop you up?
- Describe a time you felt yourself falling deeper and deeper into a pit?
- What parts of Psalm 40 struck a chord with you?

Respond

Take a few minutes to talk with God about what is stirring in your heart. Do you need to ask Him to call you out onto the water? Maybe He already has, and you just need to ask Him to give you the courage to step out of the boat. If you are sinking right now, He is ready to scoop you up. Admit to whatever is keeping you from crying out to Him and lay it at the foot of the cross. He is bigger than it all. Meditate on the ways your Father has already lifted you out of the pit and praise Him for His goodness to you.

Chapter six

wait well

wait well

Sometimes living a life of surrender means giving something up we already have, but sometimes it means finding purpose and peace in the things we don't have.

I've been avoiding writing about this part of my story – and revealing more of my heart – for the last five chapters, but I clearly know my Father is asking me to do it.

So, here I go.

It's about my singleness.

For those of you who aren't single and are about to skip this chapter because it doesn't relate to you, hold on a minute. It's not just my singleness I'm writing about, it's the reality of painfully waiting on our Father's timing, and I know everyone can relate.

Maybe you are waiting to have a job you truly love and care about. Maybe you are waiting for the season of financial havoc to be put to rest. Maybe you are waiting on someone in your life to find healing or discover a steady and sure path. Maybe you are looking for that steady and sure path. Maybe you are waiting to have a baby. Maybe you are waiting for life to finally start looking up. Maybe, like me, you are waiting for your person to come into your life.

I don't know what you are waiting for, but I can agree with you on one thing – waiting is the worst.

SOMETIMES LIVING A LIFE OF SURRENDER
MEANS GIVING SOMETHING UP WE ALREADY HAVE,
BUT SOMETIMES IT MEANS FINDING PURPOSE
AND PEACE IN THE THINGS WE DON'T HAVE.

———

Some days I find this great wave of faith to ride on and with a genuine smile on my face I can say I trust God, trust His timing, and can patiently wait in this season until He brings me the man I am praying for. And then other days, there is no wave of faith, and I find myself nearly drowning from exhaustion of trying to trust, be content, and wait.

Here's my reality: I'm single with no "maybe" guys on the horizon and as the months and years have passed, one friend after another has found their person, gotten married, and I'm about to be the only one left.

Yep, waiting is the worst.

You know by now that pride is my thorn. That I hate admitting to struggling and always want to thrive no matter the circumstance. I have always been the girl who was full of joy and found purpose in every season. I don't admit to being anything less than full of faith and thankful for the season I am in.

So, saying this to all of you is not easy…I am tired of being single. And yes, lots of the time it makes me really sad and frustrated.

Back when I was in my early teenage years, I decided for myself I wasn't going to date until I was eighteen. I thought boys were kind of dumb, thought high school relationships were pretty futile, and had no interest in flings. I just thought it made more sense to wait until I was a little older and had more of an idea about where my life was going.

The summer of my high school graduation, on a girls' trip to the lake, I told my friends I thought I would have a boyfriend by December (of 2013). Yes, go ahead and laugh.

I was sure because I was now open to dating, and was going to a Christian university, I was bound to meet the guy of my dreams right away. I mean that is how it works in Hallmark movies, right?

Well, three years went by…and nothing. Knowing I was moving back to Colorado once I graduated, I convinced myself God was waiting to put the right person in my life until I had moved back. That made sense to me, so I was okay with it.

In 2016 I graduated and moved back to Colorado. I immediately started working to find a church home and get connected. Church after church…one young adult group after the other…and nothing.

"Oh, God is just waiting for me to get settled."

"There is some growing I need to do before the right person can come along."

"I wouldn't even have time for a relationship right now."

"Maybe if I stop looking for him or thinking about it, God will make it happen."

With one "reason" after the other circling through my mind, I found myself constantly trying to make sense of why my Father hadn't brought along the right person.

Being as logical as I am, if I can find a good reason for something, I can be content, so over the years I have grasped at any possible reason as to why I am still the single one.

Those "reasons" above are only a few of them.

The reality is not only am I not married, I have never been in a relationship.

I won't bore you with all the details, but from the time I decided I wanted to wait to date until I was older, I also began praying God would guide me so I wouldn't waste time, energy, and emotions on a relationship that wasn't worth it. I wanted my every moment to count for Him, and so I didn't want to get distracted by some boy who wasn't going to be a part of my future.

Every time someone came along, I would pray and ask God to show me if this was "the person" who was worth the investment. I prayed for protection and wisdom and over and over, He made it clear this wasn't a relationship I needed to step into.

So, one awkward first date after the other, here I am.

And yes, I truly have had some very awkward dates. There was one "gentleman" who told me it was "probably a good idea" to just get water when we met at a coffee shop. Then there was the guy who showed up really late and then proceeded to stop me in the middle of talking so he could take a few minutes to respond to an email. And then there's the guy who never even made it to the first date because after being given my number his first text to me said, "Hey QT".

A few years ago, I was in one of those seasons where all I could think about was my singleness and I decided I couldn't take it anymore. I began praying fervently for God to show me my purpose in this season and help me be content.

He did just that.

I began to see the true gift of singleness and the power it had.

I saw the gift of time I had to pour into so many other relationships and serve others. I found freedom in truly establishing who I am and how I want to live my life. I traveled and had the busiest of schedules. I found the gift of being able to invest in my family in a way I know I won't' be able to do forever.

I found purpose in the singleness, and it was so freeing.

I rode that wave for a long time.

But eventually, the wave died.

And here I am – feeling vulnerable and frustrated with the timing of my Father's plans.

I feel like I've ridden every wave of faith for as long as I could. I've gone through every reason possible to defend why I'm still in this place. I've gotten as much satisfaction and joy as I can from this season. And now I'm just done with it.

Anyone else feel me on this?

You get to a place where you're just done.

On the brink of a mental breakdown where you indulge in all the good foods, cry all the tears, and quite honestly, begin to lose faith in His plans.

I feel like I'm holding on to the last thread of my hope in this situation. Because I know my Father is good, I know His plans are perfect, and so I'm fighting for those truths to be enough. But truly, I'm barely hanging on.

And I have a notion that whether or not you are feeling like this right now, you have felt like you are "barely hanging on" at some point in your past or will feel it in the coming years. Because waiting is inevitable.

It is a common thread that weaves throughout the whole Bible story.

From the beginning of creation, God's people had to wait on His plans because with a life of surrender to Him, waiting is guaranteed.

Let's look at Noah who was charged with the task of building a giant ark to live on when the flood came, yet prior to the flood, it had never even rained on Earth. While there is no answer around the exact time frame between God telling Noah to build the ark and the actual flood coming, we know it was a very long time. So here Noah was, being rejected by everyone around him for sounding like some crazy guy, claiming a flood was coming when they had never seen a drop of rain. I can't imagine the frustration Noah felt every day.

"God, I am being obedient and doing what you called me to do even to the point of losing my reputation. I have worked tirelessly on this project. Where is this flood of Yours? Why are You taking so long?"

Yet, look what is written about Noah.

"And Noah did all that the Lord commanded him."

Genesis 7:5

And because of Noah's obedience in the midst of waiting, we all know how the rest of the story goes...the flood comes, Noah, his family, and two of each animal are saved.

God starts over and promises to never flood the earth again.

The waiting was worth it.

Then there's Abraham and Sarah. They so desperately want children and God has told Abraham that his descendants will be more numerous than the stars. As time goes on both Abraham and Sarah are becoming quite old and begin to believe it is too late, so they take things into their own hands. Sarah tells Abraham to go have a child with Hagar.

> *"Now Sarai, Abram's wife, had borne him no children. But she had an Egyptian slave named Hagar; so she said to Abram, 'The Lord has kept me from having children. Go, sleep with my slave; perhaps I can build a family through her.'*
>
> *Abram agreed to what Sarai said. So after Abram had been living in Canaan ten years, Sarai his wife took her Egyptian slave Hagar and gave her to her husband to be his wife. He slept with Hagar, and she conceived."*

Genesis 16:1-4

Ultimately, Sarah becomes pregnant and gives birth to Isaac. Abraham becomes the father of many nations (through both sons), and his descendants are too many to count.

God came through.

Then, if we fast-forward to the last page of the Old Testament, we find silence – God's silence.

FOR 400 YEARS.

Let that sink in.

Generation after generation went by without hearing from God.

God had promised to send a Messiah to His people. The Israelites have escaped Egypt, wandered for forty years, made it to the land of Canaan, and have become the strong Nation God promised, only to be exiled by the Babylonians. Eventually those who wanted to return made it back, and then…silence.

There were multiple generations who were told of God's promise to send a Messiah, and after waiting their whole life, never saw the promise come to fruition.

Can you imagine?

How would you feel if what God had promised you never came to fruition in your lifetime? Be honest.

It's terrible to think about, right? Because the reality of my Father never coming through on this desire to be married is heartbreaking.

What is it that would break your heart if God didn't provide it in your lifetime? Never finding financial freedom? Never seeing that relationship restored? Never having that baby? Never finding a job you love? Never finding the physical healing you were hoping for?

The idea of that stings.

But, when we reach the New Testament, we see that God does follow through on His promise to send a Messiah. It's just a LOT later than expected and a lot different than they all anticipated.

And right there, that's life.

Almost always, God has different timing and a different delivery method than we anticipate.

The Messiah, Jesus, came just as God had promised. From the lineage of David, born to a virgin, in the town of Bethlehem. God had it planned out perfectly.

God has the answer to your promise planned out perfectly, too.

It just may look different or happen at a different time than you expected.

The plans we make on our own are nothing but futile. Our knowledge around what makes sense and what is best for us is only a sliver compared to the whole picture God is able to see. He is a faithful God. He follows through on His promises, always.

We also have to be careful that, in the midst of our wanting and waiting, we are seeking His will for our life. That we are still choosing a life of surrender.

Confession time: I thought waiting well would bring about the answer to my prayer sooner.

Have you ever felt this way?

I've tried to find reasons for why my Father hasn't placed the right man in my path. At the same time, I've made up a checklist of personal growth measures I feel I need to accomplish in order to show God I'm ready for the guy.

"If I have a good attitude about being single..."

"If I learn how to find joy in this season…"

"If I seek my Father more and use this time to grow my faith and prepare to be a wife…"

"If I serve others during this time of singleness…"

"If I fight the envy that wants to find a place in my heart…"

"If I support my friends who have what I want…"

"If I stop looking and trying…"

Then, my Father will bring me my husband.

Reality check: It doesn't work that way.

You cannot earn your way into the promises of God.

He calls on us to seek Him, serve Him, and love Him. He also promises us that His plans for us are good and we need to just trust.

Every time a friend starts dating someone, gets married, or has a baby, where malice and envy want to grow, I fight it. I fight it hard, and instead, do everything I can to let joy reside in that area of my heart.

YOU CANNOT EARN YOUR WAY
INTO THE PROMISES OF GOD.

I lean into their excitement, take my sadness out of the equation, and choose to support them in this new chapter of their life with everything I've got.

But don't let me give you the wrong impression. I don't do this seamlessly or without a fight. I am constantly doing my best to silence the voices of envy that try to convince me why I am more deserving than that friend.

"Come on Morgan, you know you deserve the man of your dreams more than she does. You have waited far better – and longer – than she has."

Malice and envy are very real and active voices from the enemy we must fight.

The minute I begin to hear those voices creep in, I make a conscious decision to pray against them. The natural tendency is to put the spotlight on myself and my unmet desires, but I fight the tendency and put the spotlight on celebrating this friend and their new blessing.

Yes, it gets exhausting because I feel like I've done this for so many years and all I can think is – when will it be my turn?

But I find if I let myself go down that path, it only leads to bitterness, frustration, and jealousy. All things that are not from Him.

So instead, I walk the opposite direction – up. It takes more effort and energy, but I choose over and over again to fight for joy for others and myself.

Which direction are you walking?

Take a minute and think about that person in your life right now who seems to have gotten what you wanted.

Are your thoughts taking you down to a place of jealousy, or are you fighting to walk up in a constant effort to celebrate that friend and trust God in His perfect timing?

If you are walking up, well done my friend, keep walking.

If you are headed down, allowing the voices of the enemy to speak to your doubt and unmet desires, start fighting.

And the only way I have found to fight is through prayer.

Begin praying fervently against the voices of the enemy. Ask God to expose the lies you believe and when they begin to show up, command them to go.

Invite Jesus in.

Ask your Father to flood your heart with belief and faith in Him that He will meet your greatest desires and needs in His perfect ways. That He will fill you with joy for others and joy for the season you are in.

That He would show you how you can serve and celebrate those friends who have what you want.

Fight to find joy for those who have what you want.

So, if it's true that waiting is a part of life and our Father often meets our desires in a different way, and at a different time than we are expecting or wanting, where do we go from here?

When we are stuck in the season of waiting to see His promises fulfilled, what do we do?

How do we wait well?

• • •

When I think about waiting, I think about David.

He started as a shepherd and ended up becoming a king.

He was described in the Bible as "a man after God's own heart."

He, who not only waited, but waited well.

It all begins when God charges Samuel with the task of finding a king. He goes off to the house of Jesse and when asked to bring all of his sons to Samuel, Jesse brings all but one. None of these boys are who Samuel is looking for, so he asks Jesse if these are all of them. Jesse replies, "Oh yeah, I do have one more who is with the sheep, but you don't want to meet him. Surely he isn't the one you are looking for."

David is called in from the fields and upon seeing him, Samuel knows David is to be king…eventually.

"So he sent for him and had him brought in. He was glowing with health and had a fine appearance and handsome features.

Then the Lord said, 'Rise and anoint him; this is the one.'

So Samuel took the horn of oil and anointed him in the presence of his brothers, and from that day on the Spirit of the Lord came powerfully upon David. Samuel then went to Ramah."

1 Samuel 16:12-13

David is believed to have been in his early teenage years at this time.

Can you imagine? David is a typical teenage boy who tends to sheep day after day. He has a house full of older brothers, which I'm sure leaves him feeling forgotten much of the time. And now he has been told he will be king.

There it is…the promise from God.

So I'm sure, like any of us would do, the minute David hears that, he assumes his whole life is about to shift from right under him. The chariots are on their way now. They will raise him up. Parade him around. Place the crown on his head. Feasts will be thrown for him. Lavish parties. Everything is about to change…

And then, it doesn't.

Nothing changes. David is told he will be king, and then almost immediately everyone disperses, and he is told to go back to tending to the sheep.

Talk about disappointment.

I know we've all been there at one time or another. You experience a moment where God speaks something so clearly to you, you assume everything is about to change, the excitement builds, your imagination plans out how it's all going to happen, you wait and wait and wait…and nothing. Everything goes back to normal, and you wonder if you even heard God correctly.

I can't be sure of it, but I would assume David is standing out in the fields day after day after day trying to sort out what Samuel had said and how he was still spending his days with the sheep. Every morning he probably waited and wondered if today was the day something would happen, and yet, nothing did happen. David tended to his sheep for many more years and just waited.

The Bible doesn't tell us what David said or thought during this season of waiting, but we do know one thing: in his season of silence and waiting, David was obedient to the task God put in front of him at that moment.

I know if I were David, I would have been trying to figure out why God had me hanging out with sheep if I was supposed to be a king. The waiting didn't make sense.

Even so, David stayed put, and carried out the task that was right in front of him.

For days and years on end, David tended to his sheep while waiting to see God move. He chose to surrender to the ultimate destination God had for him, but also, he surrendered to the path he needed to take to get there.

Eventually David begins to make a name for himself. When asked by his father to bring his brothers food in the midst of the battle they were fighting, David ends up being the only one brave enough to fight Goliath. With a slingshot and a stone, he defeats the giant.

"As the Philistine moved closer to attack him, David ran quickly toward the battle line to meet him. Reaching into his bag and taking out a stone, he slung it and struck the Philistine on the forehead. The stone sank into his forehead, and he fell face down on the ground."

1 Samuel 17:48-49

And there, on that battlefield, is the second time David is really recognized by others.

After that, through God's divine plan, David begins to play the harp for the king.

Finally, he is in the palace. Finally, he is getting somewhere.

And just as soon as David begins to believe God really might be paving the way for him to become king, David has to flee because the king wants to kill him.

There he was, in the palace, so much closer to God's anointed declaration becoming a reality, and now he was running in the opposite direction. With each step, I'm sure David felt defeat and began to wonder if God's promise was ever going to happen.

"I'm back to square one."

That's what I always say in those moments where it feels like I've just lost all the traction I had been making towards the promise.

I meet a guy, think he's great, timidly begin to think there's a chance of something happening, and then in an instant, the whole thing has ended and I'm back to the beginning.

Back to square one.

I know you've been there. A relationship you've been working to mend explodes because of a recent argument. Just as soon as you begin to catch up on paying your bills, financial hardship strikes again. The minute you begin to believe you are on a path towards doing something you love, the job offer falls through. The house doesn't sell. The cancer is back. Your child makes another reckless decision.

Yet in these "square one" moments, we get to decide how we are going to respond. Are we going to fight to believe His promises are real and choose to trust Him, or are we going to give into all the questions of disbelief we want to ask? Are we going to keep living a life of surrender to Him?

This is where the enemy prowls. He knows your hope just got crushed. He knows you are wondering where God is. He knows you are weary of fighting.

Here we must fight against all temptation to decide our Father doesn't see us and won't prove to be faithful. Here is where we have to fight against the tendency to close our fists and cling tightly to any control we can find.

In this moment, I believe the only thing to do is put our head down, flood our minds with Scripture, proclaim over and over the many times He has proved to be faithful, and never stop talking to Him.

We need to keep Him in every part of our lives, in every conversation, and in every thought.

Because where He is, the enemy has no place.

So, when I'm feeling like I'm back to "square one," I just lean in.

Head down.

Heart up.

Leaning into His promises, His word, and His goodness in my life.

We all know what happens with David – eventually. He becomes one of the greatest kings ever.

At the age of 30, many years after being told by Samuel he was going to be king, it happened.

In God's perfect timing. In His perfect way.

All those years God was preparing David and preparing the way for him.

In the same way God was preparing His people for the Messiah and the perfect way for Jesus to come into the world.

In the same way He is preparing you for this next season and making sure everything and everyone else is in the perfect place.

When we choose a life of surrender to the King, we can't just surrender to the end goal; we must surrender to the path it takes to get there. Each and every step. Moment by moment. All the days of our life.

Sometimes it feels unbearable. Sometimes it makes no sense. And sometimes it includes a season of waiting.

Waiting is inevitable, but how we choose to wait is up to us.

WAITING IS INEVITABLE,
BUT HOW WE CHOOSE
TO WAIT IS UP TO US.

Take a Minute

Remember

- Sometimes living a life of surrender means giving something up we already have, but sometimes it means finding purpose and peace in the things we don't have.
- Almost always, God has different timing and a different delivery method than we anticipate.
- God has the answer to your promise planned out perfectly.
- You cannot earn your way into the promises of God.
- Malice and envy are very real and active voices from the enemy we must fight.
- Waiting is inevitable, but how we choose to wait is up to us.

Recite

"And Noah did all that the Lord commanded him."

Genesis 7:5

"Now Sarai, Abram's wife, had borne him no children. But she had an Egyptian slave named Hagar; so she said to Abram, 'The Lord has kept me from having children. Go, sleep with my slave; perhaps I can build a family through her.'

Abram agreed to what Sarai said. So after Abram had been living in Canaan ten years, Sarai his wife took her Egyptian slave Hagar and gave her to her husband to be his wife. He slept with Hagar, and she conceived."

Genesis 16:1-4

"So he sent for him and had him brought in. He was glowing with health and had a fine appearance and handsome features.

Then the Lord said, 'Rise and anoint him; this is the one.'

So Samuel took the horn of oil and anointed him in the presence of his brothers, and from that day on the Spirit of the Lord came powerfully upon David. Samuel then went to Ramah."

1 Samuel 16:12-13

"As the Philistine moved closer to attack him, David ran quickly toward the battle line to meet him. Reaching into his bag and taking out a stone, he slung it and struck the Philistine on the forehead. The stone sank into his forehead, and he fell facedown on the ground."

1 Samuel 17:48-49

Reflect

- What are you waiting on?
- How would you feel if what you believe God has promised you never came to fruition in your lifetime? Be honest.
- Have you ever tried to earn for yourself the promise(s) you've received from God?
- Who is that person in your life who seems to have gotten what you wanted? Are your thoughts about them, taking you down to

a place of jealousy, or are you fighting to walk up in a constant effort to celebrate that friend and trust God in His perfect timing?

- When you are in the midst of waiting to see His promises fulfilled, how do you wait? With patience and a thankful heart or do you grumble and try to take matters into your own hands?

Respond

Take a few minutes to talk with God about what is stirring in your heart. Tell Him exactly what it is you are waiting on and how you feel about it. Tell Him your fears around it. Ask Him to refine your heart so your desires will line up with His will for your life. Pray for joy, purpose, and patience in this season of waiting, and ask Him to silence the enemy voices and rid your heart of all envy and anger. Thank Him for the ways He has moved, is moving, and will continue to move on the promise He has given you.

Chapter seven

no matter what

no matter what

With tears streaming down my face, I uttered this prayer.

Father, I've been obedient. I've given up everything for You. I've been patient. I've had a good attitude. Where are the blessings? I'm tired of waiting.

Finally. I had done it. I found the courage to be honest with myself and with my Father.

My prayer continued…

You asked me to give up my dream job. Financial security. A schedule that allowed for lots of travel. I did it. Where is the fruit?

I've tried to be patient in the area of dating. To be wise with my emotions and time. To honor You in all my decisions. To utilize this time of singleness to serve and grow closer to You.

While all my friends have found their person, gotten married, had babies, bought homes…I have tried to be their biggest supporter. To set aside any feelings of envy or sadness and celebrate them.

But when will it be my turn?

I always thought You promised me a husband, but now I'm losing faith. Are You actually preparing anyone for me?

Seriously, God?

All my life I wanted to be a teacher, a wife, and a mom and currently, while trying to walk obediently down a path You called me to walk, all three of those things seem to have been stripped from me or they are far from my reach.

I'm tired of fighting. I'm tired of trying to convince myself all Your plans are good. I'm tired of pretending like I'm okay.

• • •

A friend asked me the other day how my writing was going, and I told her I was uninspired, and therefore, not writing.

The truth is I don't feel put-together enough to be offering up any advice or words of encouragement to anyone.

But, as another friend pointed out, I'm pretty sure this is exactly the condition God wants me writing in.

Raw. Vulnerable. Honest. Human. Hurting. Broken. Disappointed. Tired.

I seem to think I need to have all the answers and success stories lined up and confirmed in order to stand before you and give a testimony when the reality is that the most powerful testimony of who He is comes when we, as His children, can sit in our most broken state and have the courage to share how desperate we are for Him to move.

Faith isn't inspired in others through successful people becoming successful.

Faith is inspired in others through broken people finding healing.

I know who my Savior is. I know Whose I am and who I am. I know I was created with intention and purpose. I know true satisfaction, peace, and joy can only be found in Him.

I know all the right answers.

The real problem is: What do I do when knowing the right answers isn't enough?

THE MOST POWERFUL TESTIMONY OF WHO HE IS COMES WHEN WE AS HIS CHILDREN, CAN SIT IN OUR MOST BROKEN STATE AND HAVE THE COURAGE TO SHARE HOW DESPERATE WE ARE FOR HIM TO MOVE.

Maybe you know exactly what I'm talking about.

You know who God is. You know He satisfies all of our longings. You know you should read the Bible, be in fellowship, pray, and invest in your faith. But even then, that's not enough.

Knowing the answers just isn't enough.

And that drives me insane. I'm a doer and a fixer. If there is a formula to fixing my feelings, turning things around, and making life better, I will do it.

But as I'm now realizing, sometimes following a formula of steps doesn't equal a healed heart.

Sometimes a methodical, straightforward fight isn't enough. Sometimes you need to dig deep, expose the ugly, and flat-out wage war.

As I spewed all my innermost thoughts, fears, questions, doubts, and frustrations to my friend, she gently pointed out it seemed like I was finally coming to a place of honesty…with the people in my life, with myself, and with my Father.

I was finally able to voice my biggest fears. I had thought I was brave to ignore them and claim my faith was so strong I had no need to fear. But, in all reality, I was scared to come face to face with them. I was scared to truly look them in the eye. Because what if these fears come true? What do I do then?

What if I'm single forever?

What if I never get to be a mom?

What if I don't impact enough lives?

What if I don't make a big enough mark for the Kingdom?

What if I miss out?

What if I surrender to His plans and they really aren't all that satisfying and I end up at the end of my life with unmet desires, hopes, and dreams?

What then?

What are your big "what if" questions that are scary to consider? Where are you desperate to see Him move?

FAITH ISN'T INSPIRED IN
OTHERS THROUGH PEOPLE
BECOMING SUCCESSFUL.
FAITH IS INSPIRED IN
OTHERS THROUGH BROKEN
PEOPLE FINDING HEALING.

. . .

The New Testament begins with the story of Zechariah and his wife Elizabeth. They were in their later years of life and were childless. During those times, being barren was understood to be a punishment, so I can only imagine the sorrow and shame Zechariah and Elizabeth often felt.

Yet, even in the midst of that confusion, frustration, and sorrow, look at how the Bible describes them.

"Both of them were righteous in the sight of God, observing all the Lord's commands and decrees blamelessly."

Luke 1:6

In the middle of waiting to have a child, waiting to "fit in" with society, wondering if God saw them, questioning if His plans were really good and perfect, they lived a life that honored and glorified Him.

While they were not without sin, they obeyed the commands He had given them and ultimately were seen as "righteous in the sight of God."

They served Him, loved Him, and honored Him even though He hadn't given them what they were wanting.

One day, while Zechariah was burning incense, an angel appeared and told him their waiting was finally over.

"Do not be afraid, Zechariah; your prayer has been heard. Your wife Elizabeth will bear you a son, and you are to call him John. He will be a joy and delight to you, and many will rejoice because of his birth, for he

159

will be great in the sight of the Lord. He is never to take wine or other fermented drink, and he will be filled with the Holy Spirit even before he is born. He will bring back many of the people of Israel to the Lord their God. And he will go on before the Lord, in the spirit and power of Elijah, to turn the hearts of the parents to their children and the disobedient to the wisdom of the righteous —to make ready a people prepared for the Lord."'

Luke 1:13-17

Nine months later, Elizabeth gave birth to John who prepared the way for our Savior.

Zechariah and Elizabeth could not change, speed up, or dictate His plans, but they did get to choose how they lived in the midst of waiting and wondering. They got to choose how they surrendered to His will each and every day.

They didn't let their human emotions of frustration, sadness, and confusion dictate how they worshiped, honored, and loved their Creator.

Instead, in spite of all those real and acceptable human emotions, they worshiped, honored, and loved their Creator.

They chose to wait by serving Him. By seeking Him. By being obedient to His commands.

They chose to lean into the only One who could offer them peace in a time of frustration and sadness.

They chose to wait well.

...

Abraham and Sarah had been promised a child by God and had been waiting for a long time to see the fruition of that promise.

In Genesis 17 God tells Abraham, *"I will bless her [Sarah] and will surely give you a son by her. I will bless her so that she will be the mother of nations; kings of peoples will come from her."*

And what does Abraham do?

"Abraham fell facedown; he laughed and said to himself, 'Will a son be born to a man a hundred years old? Will Sarah bear a child at the age of ninety?"

Abraham and Sarah never imagined having a child in their old age, but God was faithful to fulfill His promises and in Genesis 21 Sarah gives birth to a baby boy they name Isaac.

Honestly, sometimes I wish the story stopped there – God fulfilled His promise and their little family lived happily ever after.

The End.

But if you've read further in Genesis, you know the story continues.

Genesis 22 starts off with, *"Some time later God tested Abraham. He said to him, 'Abraham!'*

'Here I am,' he replied.

Then God said, 'Take your son, your only son, Isaac, whom you love, and go to the region of Moriah. Sacrifice him there as a burnt offering on one of the mountains I will show you.'"

Every time I read this part of the story, a little pit forms in my stomach and I get uncomfortable. I've never liked to process the reality of this request from God and years back I went through a season where I found myself feeling really upset at God for asking Abraham to do this.

How dare He promise Abraham and Sarah a child, make them wait so long to see that promise fulfilled, to then come back years later asking Abraham to kill his son.

When I think of my Heavenly Father, He makes me feel safe, loved, valued, and protected.

But when I think of my Heavenly Father asking Abraham to sacrifice his own son, those feelings fall away into a dark abyss.

I know the reason this story brings me so much discomfort is because I fear that in the same way God asked Abraham to sacrifice someone so dear to him, God might ask me to do the same. That part of surrendering my plans might mean losing someone or something I love.

What if I lose someone I love in an accident? What if a relationship in my life gets destroyed? What if I can't live as close to my family as I want to? What if the thing I am waiting on never comes to fulfillment?

What if God asks me to sacrifice the thing nearest to my heart?

Could I still think of Him and feel safe, loved, valued, and protected? Would I obey Him? Would I still choose to follow Him?

What is nearest to your heart? What if in surrendering to His will, God asked you to sacrifice that? Would you choose to obey? Would you still choose to follow Him?

What does Abraham decide to do?

The next morning, he gets up, gathers wood, and has two of his servants and Isaac set out with him to the place God told him to go.

He obeys.

The Bible doesn't give us insight into Abraham's inner dialogue and feelings, but I wish it did.

I would love to know how Abraham was processing through this direction from God.

Was he angry? Confused? Heartbroken? Trusting? Calm?

My guess is he felt all of these things.

I assume he cycled through these feelings over and over like a pinball machine. Wrestling to balance the feelings of wanting to trust God but also feeling so confused and hurt by this request.

Yet, no matter the feelings he felt or the things he thought, he obeyed God's direction.

His experiences had taught Him that the only life worth living was one of obedience to God's voice.

Whether that voice was telling him what he wanted to hear or not, He chose to honor it above all else.

And in the end? God honored that obedience and told Abraham, *"...because you have done this and have not withheld your son, your only son, I will surely bless you and make your descendants as numerous as the stars in the sky and as the sand on the seashore."*

In the midst of confusion, fear, and doubt, Abraham obeyed the voice of the One he knew would never lead him astray.

• • •

When all was lost, Ruth chose to respond with grace, obedience, and sacrifice.

In the first chapter of the book of Ruth we are introduced to three widows – Naomi and her two daughters-in-law, Orpah and Ruth. After losing their husbands, they all have to decide what next steps to take and how they are going to survive this next season.

Naomi decides to return home to Bethlehem and urges Orpah and Ruth to return to their homes to Moab in hopes of a better future for both of them.

"Go back, each of you, to your mother's home. May the Lord show you kindness, as you have shown kindness to your dead husbands and to me. May the Lord grant that each of you will find rest in the home of another husband."

Ruth 1:8-9

Orpah agrees to return home to Moab, but Ruth insists she will stay with Naomi and go to Bethlehem.

"Don't urge me to leave you or to turn back from you. Where you go I will go, and where you stay I will stay. Your people will be my people and your God my God. Where you die I will die, and there I will be buried. May the Lord deal with me, be it ever so severely, if even death separates you and me."

Ruth 1:16-17

After reaching Bethlehem, Ruth recognizes the need to care for her mother-in-law. She learns more about Naomi's family and about a man of importance among them named Boaz. Ruth asks permission to gather leftover grains from his field for their sustenance.

In very little time, Boaz notices Ruth, and knowing what she had done to serve and love Naomi, he does all he can to keep her safe and provide for them. The book of Ruth goes on to tell the story of Boaz and Ruth eventually getting married.

At first glance, the short story of Ruth is easily passed by without much notice, but when we take a second to truly read the story and recognize the heart of Ruth and the choices she makes, we can find such incredible direction and guidance when it comes to living a life of surrender.

As a woman in Bible times, you had very little value without your husband. So not only does Ruth lose her husband, but she also loses her security and identity. She is left with nothing and chooses to follow a woman who has also been left with nothing.

The easiest and seemingly most beneficial choice for her was to return to her home, Moab, to be with her family in hopes of finding a new husband. Instead, she recognizes the needs of Naomi and chooses to put those before her own.

Ruth CHOOSES to go to a foreign land, which means giving up her gods and adopting Naomi's. She CHOOSES to sacrifice for the well-being of Naomi who is full of bitterness. She CHOOSES serving over comfort and ease.

In a society that didn't ask or expect this of her, Ruth exemplifies the boldness and courage it takes to respond well when her life fell apart. When her life didn't go as she planned.

Rather than trying to make choices that would rebuild her life and grant her a promising future, she makes the choice to surrender to His will and be obedient to what God had put right in front of her, trusting He would take care of the rest.

If I put myself in Ruth's shoes, the minute my future and life crumbled, my first response would have been to map out the choices I needed to make to rebuild my life. I would have grasped for any sense of control and scrambled to make sense of it all.

My first response would not have been to look to someone else's crumbled life and decide what I could do to help rebuild theirs first.

All too often my first instinct is to improve my life instead of improving the lives of those around me.

What I've learned from the story of Ruth is that when I choose to serve who is right in front of me and be obedient with what God has placed in my hands, He will sort out my life. And He will do the same for you.

Is there a friend who needs practical support right now – such as having a meal delivered to them or a day where someone watches their children? Could you set aside twenty minutes and call someone who needs encouragement? Does your neighbor need their yard mowed? Is there a ministry in your church in need of volunteers?

When we choose to put serving His Kingdom above building ours, He provides a future for us that is more than we could ever ask for or imagine.

I believe that after years of hearing about Naomi's God, Ruth believed in Him too. That in a season of waiting, confusion, and loss, Ruth trusted He would take care of her – that He would provide for both her and Naomi – and that He had good and perfect plans for her future.

————

WHEN WE CHOOSE TO PUT SERVING HIS KINGDOM ABOVE BUILDING OURS, HE PROVIDES A FUTURE FOR US THAT IS MORE THAN WE COULD EVER ASK OR IMAGINE.

————

And in the end, because of Ruth's choices, Boaz is brought into her life and God grants her the desires of her heart.

He meets her needs because she decided to help meet the needs of others.

• • •

The most well-known man in the Bible for having his world turned upside down is Job.

In the first verse of the book of Job, he is described as being blameless, upright, fearing God, and shunning evil. A few verses later he is called "the greatest man among all the people of the East."

Whenever I run across descriptions of someone's character in the Bible, my immediate reaction is to think, "If I was included in the Bible, what words would be used to describe me?"

Talk about a solid attitude check.

In Job's case, he was clearly a very respected man who lived in a way that was consistent with God's law.

Well, one day, as Satan was roaming the earth, God pointed Job out to him saying, *"Have you considered my servant Job? There is no one on earth like him; he is blameless and upright, a man who fears God and shuns evil."*

Does that hit you smack in the face the same way it does me? Can you imagine God describing you in this way?

What a remarkable benchmark to live by, always thinking – how would God describe me in this moment?

Well, seeing that Job was such an outstanding man, Satan decides he is going to attack Job and his life by taking away all the things that mattered most to him. In no time at all, Job loses his sheep, oxen, camels, donkeys, servants – and all his sons and daughters.

He loses everything.

> *"At this, Job got up and tore his robe and shaved his head."*

> Job 1:20

This act signifies incredible grief and mourning.

Can you relate?

Stop for a minute and think back to a moment where you felt this way. Where you felt you had lost everything or maybe a moment where you felt you had nothing. One of those days, weeks, or months where it felt like everything was falling apart. Where your world was crumbling around you.

When you find yourself in this space, don't run from it. Don't rush it. Don't ignore it. Allowing yourself to feel during this season – to grieve and to mourn – is incredibly necessary and one step closer towards a healed heart.

Maybe you are feeling that right now. Like the ground beneath you might give way at any moment.

Find comfort, my friend, in knowing you are not alone in feeling this way. Job felt it, Jesus felt it before His crucifixion, and we all have experienced it.

So, when the floods of tragedy and trials come our way, what do we do?

> *"Then he [Job] fell to the ground in worship and said, 'Naked I came from my mother's womb, and naked I will depart. The Lord gave and the Lord has taken away; may the name of the Lord be praised.' In all this, Job did not sin by charging God with wrongdoing."*

Job 1:20-22

The Pulpit Commentary (edited by H. D. M. Spence and Joseph S. Exell) about this passage of Scripture says it best, "After giving vent to his natural grief, Job made an act of adoration. Recognizing the fact that adversity, as well as prosperity comes from God, and submitting himself to the Divine will, he 'worshipped.' How often has his act flashed across the minds of Christians and enabled them, in their dark hour, to imitate him, and repeat his words, 'The Lord gave.'"

I believe those statements are so true. How often do you hear people refer to themselves as feeling like Job? For so many of us, when these moments of incredible loss and tragedy come our way, we find solace in knowing that someone somewhere can relate and has gone through something similar. So, relating to the story of Job can bring comfort. Yet, how often does our comparison to his situation end there?

If we identify with Job and his story of loss, then we should also try and identify with his response.

He responded with tremendous grief, which is a natural human reaction, but from there he went straight to adoration. He got on his knees and PRAISED.

He worshipped our Father in the midst of his darkest hour.

Anyone else come to mind who did that same thing? (Hint: it's Jesus.)

> *"Then he said to them, 'My soul is very sorrowful, even to death; remain here, and watch with me.' And going a little farther he fell on his face and prayed, saying, 'My Father, if it be possible, let this cup pass from me; nevertheless, not as I will, but as you will.'"*

Matthew 26:38-39 (ESV)

Right before His crucifixion, feeling the weight of it all, Jesus cried out to God in agony, but then still chose to ultimately submit to God's sovereignty over His own desires. He knew God's will was best.

Job also recognized the goodness of our God, the sovereignty of His character, and the wonders of His plans. He chose to surrender all his pain and anger to God and submit to His plans – whatever they might be. There Job finds rest, refuge, and comfort in the arms of his good Father.

In the midst of his darkest hour, Job praised.

· · ·

When life wasn't going the way Abraham planned, he chose to surrender and obey.

When life wasn't going the way Ruth planned, she chose to surrender and serve.

When life wasn't going the way Job planned, he chose to surrender and praise.

So, what can we do if His plans really aren't all that satisfying and we end up at the end of our life with unmet desires, hopes, and dreams?

We can surrender to His will, obey His commands and follow His direction for our life.

For me personally, this looks like continuing to carve out space each morning to spend time with Him and be in His Word. It means surrounding myself with mentors, pastors, and friends who will help refine me and challenge me in becoming someone who reflects Jesus. It means asking Him what I can do to help build His Kingdom. It means asking God to show me where I can grow and what I need to change in my life.

We can serve and love those around us, pouring into the season He has us in.

Personally, this means investing in relationships He has called me to – family members, friends, and neighbors. It means supporting my friends in their growing families – praying for their marriages, loving on their babies, continuing to invest in those friendships despite all the changes. It means loving my future husband by continuing to better myself for our marriage and make choices that honor him and our future family.

And no matter what, we can praise His name because He is worthy of it all.

Some days this comes easy, and other days it doesn't, but I try my best. I find reasons to thank Him. I lift up a song to Him. I pour out my heart to Him.

Whether or not you are living a life of surrender right now, you will find yourself in a season of waiting. And when that wave of contentment dies, how will you wait? Will you wait well? In that season of waiting how can you obey? How can you serve? How can you praise?

Waiting for what we want is scary. Obeying His calling on our life isn't easy. And having faith amidst the trials doesn't always come without a fight.

But I can assure you of one thing, choosing Him above all else will never disappoint.

Let me leave you with one final thought...

An Advent study by Proverbs 31 Ministries called Pointing to the Promise says, "Although our disbelief in God's promise will not prevent Him from keeping His word, it will prevent us from experiencing peace while we wait."

Take a Minute

Remember

- The most powerful testimony of who He is comes when we, as His children, can sit in our most broken state and have the courage to share how desperate we are for Him to move.
- Faith isn't inspired in others through successful people becoming successful. Faith is inspired in others through broken people finding healing.
- Don't let your human emotions dictate how you worship your Creator.
- The only life worth living is one of obedience to God's voice.
- When we choose to put serving His Kingdom above building ours, He provides a future for us that is more than we could ever ask for or imagine.
- If we identify with Job and his story of loss, then we should also try and identify with his response.

Recite

"Both of them were righteous in the sight of God, observing all the Lord's commands and decrees blamelessly."

Luke 1:6

"Do not be afraid, Zechariah; your prayer has been heard. Your wife Elizabeth will bear you a son, and you are to call him John. He will be a joy and delight to you, and many will rejoice because of his birth, for he will be great in the sight of the Lord. He is never to take wine or other

fermented drink, and he will be filled with the Holy Spirit even before he is born. He will bring back many of the people of Israel to the Lord their God. And he will go on before the Lord, in the spirit and power of Elijah, to turn the hearts of the parents to their children and the disobedient to the wisdom of the righteous—to make ready a people prepared for the Lord.'"

Luke 1:13-17

"I will bless her and will surely give you a son by her. I will bless her so that she will be the mother of nations; kings of peoples will come from her."

Genesis 17:16

"Abraham fell facedown; he laughed and said to himself, 'Will a son be born to a man a hundred years old? Will Sarah bear a child at the age of ninety?"

Genesis 17:17

"Some time later God tested Abraham. He said to him, 'Abraham!'

'Here I am,' he replied.

Then God said, 'Take your son, your only son, Isaac, whom you love, and go to the region of Moriah. Sacrifice him there as a burnt offering on one of the mountains I will show you.'"

Genesis 22:1-2

175

"Because you have done this and have not withheld your son, your only son, I will surely bless you and make your descendants as numerous as the stars in the sky and as the sand on the seashore."

Genesis 22:16-17

"Go back, each of you, to your mother's home. May the Lord show you kindness, as you have shown kindness to your dead husbands and to me. May the Lord grant that each of you will find rest in the home of another husband."

Ruth 1:8-9

"Don't urge me to leave you or to turn back from you. Where you go I will go, and where you stay I will stay. Your people will be my people and your God my God. Where you die I will die, and there I will be buried. May the Lord deal with me, be it ever so severely, if even death separates you and me."

Ruth 1:16-17

"Have you considered my servant Job? There is no one on earth like him; he is blameless and upright, a man who fears God and shuns evil."

Job 1:8

"At this, Job got up and tore his robe and shaved his head."

Job 1:20

"Then he fell to the ground in worship and said, 'Naked I came from my mother's womb, and naked I will depart. The Lord gave and the Lord has taken away; may the name of the Lord be praised.' In all this, Job did not sin by charging God with wrongdoing."

Job 1:20-22

"Then he said to them, 'My soul is very sorrowful, even to death; remain here, and watch with me.' And going a little farther he fell on his face and prayed, saying, 'My Father, if it be possible, let this cup pass from me; nevertheless, not as I will, but as you will.'"

Matthew 26:38-39 (ESV)

Reflect

- What are your big "what if" questions that are scary to consider? Where are you desperate to see Him move?
- What is nearest to your heart? What if in surrendering to His will, God asked you to sacrifice that? How would that make you feel? Would you choose to obey?
- Despite what might be going on in your life, is God calling you to serve someone or serve somewhere right now?
- Describe a time you felt like Job? How did you choose to respond?

Respond

Take a few minutes to talk with God about what is stirring in your heart right now. Tell Him those big "what if" questions and where you are desperate to see Him move. Talk to Him about how it would make you feel if He asked you to give up the person, place, or thing nearest to your heart. Ask Him to fill you with boldness and obedience if that time ever comes. Finally, take a few minutes and think about how you have responded to seasons of waiting, frustration, or hurt in your life. Ask Him to forgive you for the times you didn't respond well and then bask in His forgiveness, grace, and mercy knowing tomorrow is a new day.

Chapter eight

send it floating

send it floating

A few weeks ago, I was leading our church in worship, and we were singing one of my favorite songs by Hillsong Worship called "New Wine."

Whenever I sing this song, my mind immediately goes to my decision to leave teaching and step into full time ministry. It puts into focus this last year of my life and the choice I made to surrender it all in belief and trust that God would bring new wine out of me. In my naive thinking, I had surrendered it all.

So, as the band rehearsed and I sang the song, I grinned as I thought about my life and how I was no longer clinging for control. I thought about how freeing that felt, and honestly, I was proud of myself for how much I had worked to overcome this part of my life...this obsession with control.

That morning, before leaving my house for church, I had written a prayer asking God to challenge me and reveal Himself to me while I worshiped.

During the first service, I sang a line that talked about the soil we surrender and how He can break new ground. Right in that moment He spoke so clearly to me.

He said, "Morgan, surrender Maliyah. Stop grasping for control. Release her to Me."

(If you don't remember, Maliyah is my sister. I talked about some of her story at the beginning of this book.)

Now, there are only a handful of times in my life I've felt my Father speak to me so clearly – and this was one of them.

In an instant, the message of that song broke me all over again.

For the rest of the morning, I couldn't shake what He had said to me.

He had just revealed to me a massive crack in my faith.

Over the last year I had done the hard work of surrendering control of MY life, but I was still holding tight to the hearts and futures of the people I loved most.

I (maybe) wasn't trying to control my life but I was definitely trying to control the lives of others. I was under the impression (which was camouflaged in helpfulness) that I had the power to heal hearts and I believed it was on me to rescue people. I had burdened myself with the task of saving those in my line of sight.

What I didn't realize was, by burdening myself with such an impossible task, I was less effective in utilizing my gifts and abilities for the sake of building His Kingdom.

"Bear one another's burdens, and so fulfill the law of Christ."

Galatians 6:2 (ESV)

There is a fine line between bearing one another's burdens and carrying one another's burdens.
Bearing is defined as "a structural part that **supports** weight, such as a wall that **supports** a beam."

Bearing someone's burdens means we step in as a support beam alongside that person to help lessen the load they are carrying on their own, all while remembering our Father is the firm foundation holding us both up.

THERE IS A FINE LINE BETWEEN BEARING ANOTHER'S BURDENS AND CARRYING ANOTHER'S BURDENS.

In Galatians 6:2, our Father isn't asking us to step in and relieve someone by trying to carry one hundred percent of someone's burden. He isn't asking us to step in and save the situation.

Instead, He is calling us to step in, and help bear the load.

Picture this...a man is standing on a firm concrete slab in mid-air. Suddenly, a ceiling is dropped down on top of him and he finds himself fighting to hold it above his head to keep it from crushing him. A friend sees him struggling under the weight and comes beside him to help bear the load. Over time, as more people see the struggle, they also step in. The more people that offer support, the lighter the load each person is carrying. And while each person is giving away some of their strength, time, and energy to help, ultimately, He is the foundation holding everyone up.

That is the intention of Galatians 6:2. That we would support one another by helping bear the weight life drops on us at different times, trusting and knowing our Father is truly carrying the weight of it all.

For too long I have been trying to carry the burdens of those I love and in doing so, I often feel overwhelmed, exhausted, and like I am letting people down.

Have you been here before, too? Does this bring to mind someone specific in your life?

We are called to serve others, not fix what's broken. That's His job.

We are called to love others, not save them. That's His job.

My love for Maliyah is beyond what I can put into words. I care about her heart and her future so much that for the last twelve years I have been trying to carry her burdens, her heart, and her hopes. I have unintentionally believed my actions possess the power to determine the course of her future and the state of her heart. The pressure I have felt has been unbearable, exhausting, and not from Him.

So, a few weeks ago, when my Father opened up my eyes to this need of not just surrendering my life to Him, but also the lives of those I love, it wrecked me.

And it's not just Maliyah I do this with, it's so many of the people I love.

I have allowed the enemy to fixate my mind on the power of ME versus the power of HE.

HE is the able One.

HE sees the need. HE sees their heart.

HE loves them more than I do.

HE has a plan.

HE will make a way.

And as for ME, rather than loving by my own strength, it's time to surrender the hearts of the people I love to Him.

———

DON'T ALLOW THE ENEMY TO FIXATE YOUR MIND ON THE POWER OF ME VERSUS THE POWER OF HE.

———

Who do you need to surrender?

Whose heart are you clinging to in hopes your actions can change the outcome?

A child? A spouse? A family member? A best friend? A significant other?

Maybe, like me, you can come up with a never ending list of people you want to impact and save.

Well, it's time to let go.

Surrendering your personal life and heart to Him is a daily choice, and so is this.

Surrendering the hearts of those you love to Him is something you have to choose to do each and every day.

You were not designed to carry the weight of anyone's future. You were designed to come alongside His children, be a beam of support, and champion them on.

As you read the following letter I wrote to Maliyah, I want you to think about that person you have been clinging to. Let this encourage you to recognize what your place in their life is and remember what role He plays in their life. Find freedom, relief, and rest in these words.

Dear Maliyah,

The other day someone asked me to describe to them my role in your life.

My answer?

I want to be your biggest cheerleader.

Yes, I strive to be the sister who fills your life with adventure, sits with you in your sorrow, and acts goofy to remind you to be yourself. I desire to be someone who speaks truth and encouragement into your life day in and day out. I hope to be someone who makes you laugh and keeps life exciting.

But more than anything, I want you to see me as your biggest cheerleader.

I want you to know that no matter what, I'm on your squad.

Good day or bad day.

Wise decision or dumb decision.

You tell me you hate me or tell me you love me.

I am going nowhere.

I may encourage you in one direction or another. I will gently counsel you when I think you are headed in the wrong direction. I'll share with you what I believe you need to hear.

But in the midst of that, I will always be on your side. Defending you. Supporting you. Loving you.

So, when you are angry and your words to me are, "Go away. I don't like you," my response will be, "I'm not going anywhere. I love you."

When you make the wrong choice and people want to remind you of your mistakes, I'll remind you of all your wins.

When you are battling to figure out who you are, I'll remind you Whose you are.

I will always be on your sidelines as you play this game called life.

I'll be the one cheering for you so loud you become slightly embarrassed, and people wonder what's wrong with me.

I'll ignore what's labeled as proper to be sure you hear my words above everyone else's…because I love you a whole lot.

But today, as I was praying for you and thinking about who I want to be to you, it hit me.

I want to be your biggest cheerleader, but I can't be…that spot is already taken.

You see your Father, our Abba, He already claimed the role as your biggest cheerleader.

The person I hope and strive to be for you…your constant, your confidant, your best friend, your counselor, your encourager…He is all of that and so much more.

HE is your biggest cheerleader.

No matter what, He is on your squad.

Good day or bad day.

Wise decision or dumb decision.

You tell Him you hate Him or tell Him you love Him.

He is going nowhere.

He will encourage you in the right direction. He will gently counsel you when He notices you are headed in the wrong direction. He will share with you what He knows you need to hear.

And in the midst of that, He will always be on your side. Defending you. Supporting you. Loving you.

So, when you are angry and your words to Him are, "Go away. I don't like you," His response will be, "I'm not going anywhere. I love you. I've always loved you and I'll never stop loving you!"

"For I am sure that neither death nor life, nor angels nor rulers, nor things present nor things to come, nor powers, nor height nor depth, nor anything else in all creation, will be able to separate us from the love of God in Christ Jesus our Lord."

Romans 8:38-39 (ESV)

When you make the wrong choice and people want to remind you of your mistakes, He will remind you of all your wins.

"For I can do everything through Christ, who gives me strength."

Philippians 4:13 (NLT)

When you are battling to figure out who you are, He will remind you who He created you to be.

"I knew you before I formed you in your mother's womb. Before you were born I set you apart...."

Jeremiah 1:5 (NLT)

He will always be on your sidelines as you play this game called life.

"Be strong and courageous. Do not be afraid or terrified because of them, for the LORD your God goes with you; he will never leave you nor forsake you."

Deuteronomy 31:6

He will be the one cheering for you so loud people wonder who this is you've got on your side.

"What then shall we say to these things? If God is for us, who can be against us?"

Romans 8:31 (ESV)

He will ignore what's labeled as proper to be sure you hear His words above everyone else's...because He loves you a whole lot.

"… And I pray that you, being rooted and established in love, may have power, together with all the Lord's holy people, to grasp how wide and long and high and deep is the love of Christ, and to know this love that surpasses knowledge – that you may be filled to the measure of all the fullness of God."

Ephesians 3:17b-19

So, my girl, know this: You've got your Heavenly Father as your number one cheerleader. And you've got your obnoxiously loud obsessive sister who comes in as a close second.

You are being championed forever and always.

Your sidelines will never ever be empty.

All my love, Morgan.

• • •

Be a cheerleader for those you love. Champion them. Serve them and love them.

But also remember, our Father is their number one fan. You don't have to try and fill that spot in their life because He already has.

The status of their heart, the healing they need, the provision they are seeking…it is not found in you or what you can offer them.

It is found in Him.

As I fight each day to surrender my life to Him, I am also fighting to surrender the hearts of those I love.

Here's one way I practice that: Each morning I get on my knees and open my hands towards heaven. Then, I unload my heart. I say out loud everything I am feeling weighed down by – things in my life and the names and needs of those I love. Afterwards, I thank Him for all He has already done, is doing, and will do in every situation and each heart I just brought to Him. I ask Him to use me, guide me, and speak through me.

And with that, my heart has been unloaded and I have put everything in His hands.

I have surrendered it all.

Doing that each morning doesn't guarantee I won't worry later that day or experience a moment of doubt, but it does start off my day with a physical act of surrender and a verbal declaration of trust.

My day is now fueled by a peace that comes from surrender rather than a fear that comes from attempted control.

———

LIVE A LIFE FUELED BY A PEACE THAT COMES FROM SURRENDER RATHER THAN A FEAR THAT COMES FROM ATTEMPTED CONTROL.

———

• • •

As I lean into this idea of surrendering those we love, I can't help but think of Moses and his mama.

Talk about a rockstar woman. She was courageous to the core.

191

Out of fear the Israelites were becoming too numerous, the Egyptians forced the Israelites into slavery. When they continued to multiply despite the Egyptians efforts to stop them, Pharaoh ordered that every boy born must be thrown into the Nile.

During that time Jochebed gave birth to Moses.

> *"Now a man of the tribe of Levi married a Levite woman, and she became pregnant and gave birth to a son. When she saw that he was a fine child, she hid him for three months. But when she could hide him no longer, she got a papyrus basket for him and coated it with tar and pitch. Then she placed the child in it and put it among the reeds along the bank of the Nile. His sister stood at a distance to see what would happen to him."*

Exodus 2:1-4

Whenever I read this passage, I picture the way this scene plays out in the movie *The Prince of Egypt*. This sweet mother desperately trying to protect her baby boy as he is hunted down by soldiers who intend to kill him. I can picture her nestling Moses under her shawl as she hears the trampling feet of soldiers nearby. By the time Moses is three months old, he becomes too loud to keep hidden and she realizes in order to save him, she must let him go.

In order to save the person you love, you must let them go.

In order to save Maliyah, I must let her go.

In order to save, _____ you must let them go. (*You fill in the blank.*)

I can't help but wonder how Jochebed came to this decision. I'm not sure what kind of clarity a mother could get in order to decide her only option of saving her son is to put him in a basket and send him floating down the Nile River.

The only answer I can come up with is that Jochebed must have had an incredibly intimate and strong relationship with God to have heard and then obeyed directions like this.

I love what the respected Christian author, Mary Elizabeth Baxter, said, "It would have been a venturesome experiment, if Jochebed had been unable to trust her God."

There's no way Jochebed would have been able to take a risk like this if she didn't have complete trust that God cared more about Moses' future than she did.

She trusted that God's plan for Moses was bigger and better than anything she could do for him, so she let him go.

You see, in order to truly surrender those we love most to the God who created them, we must know Him – personally. Because once we really know Him, we will discover He is trustworthy, He has a perfect plan for each of His children, and He is holding each one of us in the palm of His hands.

Without a personal relationship, there is no trust. And without trust, there is no surrender.

The only way Jochebed was able to take her baby boy and let him float down the Nile River in a basket was because she knew God – personally.

And the only way any of us will find that surrender for our lives, or the people we love, is if we know Him – personally.

Do you know what happened after she sent Moses floating down the Nile River?

> *"Then Pharaoh's daughter went down to the Nile to bathe, and her*
> *attendants were walking along the riverbank. She saw the basket among*
> *the reeds and sent her female slave to get it. She opened it and saw the*
> *baby. He was crying, and she felt sorry for him. 'This is one of the*
> *Hebrew babies,' she said. Then his sister asked Pharaoh's daughter,*
> *'Shall I go and get one of the Hebrew women to nurse the baby for you?'*
> *'Yes, go,' she answered. So the girl went and got the baby's mother.*
> *Pharaoh's daughter said to her, 'Take this baby and nurse him for me,*
> *and I will pay you.' So the woman took the baby and nursed him. When*
> *the child grew older, she took him to Pharaoh's daughter and he became*
> *her son. She named him Moses, saying, 'I drew him out of the water.'"*

Exodus 2:5-10

Moses found safety in the hands of Pharaoh's daughter and without them realizing who she was, Jochebed was asked to feed him.

That is the kind of provision and care God will give to all His children when they are put in His hands.

While Moses encounters his fair share of troubles and mistakes growing up, he eventually hears from God through a burning bush, and God uses him to lead the Israelites out of Egypt.

Had Jochebed not had an intimate enough relationship with God to hear His voice and direction…

Had Jochebed not surrendered her baby boy over to the God who created him…

Had Jochebed not recklessly trusted God…

Honestly, I don't know.

My mind goes to Moses being found by the Egyptian soldiers and killed. And if that happened, then what might have been the history of the Israelites and the Promised Land?

Luckily, our God is bigger than our disobedience and His plan would have prevailed no matter what...but still, look at the fruit that came from Jochebed surrendering Moses.

What fruit is waiting to grow because you haven't yet given over the hearts of someone you love to Him?

I never want Maliyah to be held back from His incredibly wonderful plans for her because I cling too tightly.

I never want my fear or lack of trust to be the reason she isn't fully leaning into the plans He has for her.

I want to recklessly trust God, like Jochebed did, and send Maliyah down the Nile River in a basket. Completely free of my grip. Totally surrendered to the work of His hands.

And for me, it's not just Maliyah I need to put in a basket and send down the Nile River.

It's all the hearts and futures of the people on my prayer lists. It's my family members. It's my dearest friends.

Believing I am the answer for any of their broken hearts or challenging situations, will only hurt me...and hurt them.

Instead, each morning as I get on my knees, I am going to take each worry, person I love, and fear I have, and pile it high in the basket. Then, with a resounding AMEN, I am going to send that basket floating down the Nile letting the waves of His perfect plans lead the way.

But I won't just do this one time, because I know that 24 hours later, I'll be trying to cling tightly again.

Instead, each morning I will choose to recklessly trust Him with those I love most.

You are not the person who can save them. You cannot heal them. You don't have the ability to fix their problems.

That's His job.

It's time to let go. It's time to trust Him.

Come on…do it with me. Fill up that basket and send it floating.

And the fruit that will come…man, oh man…it's going to be incredible.

IN ORDER TO SAVE THE
PEOPLE YOU LOVE, YOU MUST
LET THEM GO.

Take a Minute

Remember

- There is a fine line between bearing one another's burdens and carrying one another's burdens.
- Don't allow the enemy to fixate your mind on the power of ME versus the power of HE.
- You were not designed to carry the weight of anyone's future. You were designed to come alongside His children, be a beam of support, and champion them on.
- Live a life fueled by a peace that comes from surrender rather than a fear that comes from attempted control.
- In order to save the people you love, you must let them go.
- Without a personal relationship, there is no trust. And without trust, there is no surrender.

Recite

"Bear one another's burdens, and so fulfill the law of Christ."

Galatians 6:2 (ESV)

"For I am sure that neither death nor life, nor angels nor rulers, nor things present nor things to come, nor powers, nor height nor depth, nor anything else in all creation, will be able to separate us from the love of God in Christ Jesus our Lord."

Romans 8:38-39 (ESV)

"For I can do everything through Christ, who gives me strength."

Philippians 4:13 (NLT)

"I knew you before I formed you in your mother's womb. Before you were born I set you apart..."

Jeremiah 1:5 (NLT)

"Be strong and courageous. Do not be afraid or terrified because of them, for the LORD your God goes with you; he will never leave you nor forsake you."

Deuteronomy 31:6

"What then shall we say to these things? If God is for us, who can be against us?"

Romans 8:31 (ESV)

"... And I pray that you, being rooted and established in love, may have power, together with all the Lord's holy people, to grasp how wide and long and high and deep is the love of Christ, and to know this love that surpasses knowledge—that you may be filled to the measure of all the fullness of God."

Ephesians 3:17b-19

"Now a man of the tribe of Levi married a Levite woman, and she became pregnant and gave birth to a son. When she saw that he was a fine child, she hid him for three months. But when she could hide him no longer, she got a papyrus basket for him and coated it with tar and pitch. Then she placed the child in it and put it among the reeds along the bank of the Nile. His sister stood at a distance to see what would happen to him."

Exodus 2:1-4

"Then Pharaoh's daughter went down to the Nile to bathe, and her attendants were walking along the riverbank. She saw the basket among the reeds and sent her female slave to get it. She opened it and saw the baby. He was crying, and she felt sorry for him. 'This is one of the Hebrew babies,' she said.

Then his sister asked Pharaoh's daughter, 'Shall I go and get one of the Hebrew women to nurse the baby for you?'

'Yes, go,' she answered. So the girl went and got the baby's mother. Pharaoh's daughter said to her, 'Take this baby and nurse him for me, and I will pay you.' So the woman took the baby and nursed him. When the child grew older, she took him to Pharaoh's daughter and he became her son. She named him Moses, saying, 'I drew him out of the water.'"

Exodus 2:5-10

Reflect

- Do you tend to carry people's burdens rather than help bear them?
- Who do you need to surrender? Whose heart are you clinging to in hopes your actions can change the outcome?
- Do you trust God will take care of the people you love most?

- Can you think of an example in your life, or someone else's, where there was incredible fruit because someone stopped clinging too tightly to another person they loved and instead, gave God control?

Respond

Take a few minutes to talk with God about what He is stirring in your heart. Who is the person you need to surrender? Spend the next few minutes telling God how much you care for this person, what your hopes and dreams are for them. Then proclaim you trust Him with their heart and future. Ask God to show you how you can continue to love and support this person, but also ask Him to give you the strength to stop clinging.

I encourage you to end your prayer time today by getting on your knees and holding your hands open to heaven. Unload your heart. Say out loud everything (every little or big thing) you feel weighs you down. Then, thank Him for all He has already done, is doing, and will do in every situation you've given Him, and in each heart you just brought to Him.

Fill up that basket and send it floating.

Chapter nine

His ways

His ways

I wasn't planning on going to school in Tennessee.

I wasn't planning on teaching second grade or teaching at Soaring Hawk Elementary.

I wasn't planning on buying a condo in 2018.

I wasn't planning on leaving teaching four years in.

I wasn't planning on being single for this long.

I wasn't planning on leading worship and doing full-time ministry.

I wasn't planning for my life to look like this.

And yet, I can't imagine it any other way.

*"For my thoughts are not your thoughts, neither are your ways my ways,'
declares the LORD. 'As the heavens are higher than the earth, so are
my ways higher than your ways and my thoughts than your thoughts.'"*

Isaiah 55:8-9

You've probably heard this verse a million times and seen it plastered all over Hobby Lobby home decor. It's one of those Scriptures we quickly fall back on because of the hope it brings. It's an easy Scripture to turn to when your plans aren't working out and the future looks dim. It reminds us of His sovereignty in all things.

But I think all too often we read this verse in the wrong context...or at least I do.

When I hear this Scripture, the first thing it makes me feel is safe and hopeful. I think, "Yeah, God's got my back. It's all good."

Here's what I mean: my initial feelings when I hear this verse are always centered around good things happening in my life – blessings I don't deserve or seasons of surprise and delight I wasn't expecting. Everything I relate this verse to is from a perspective of comfort and ease...all the good parts of life.

Like the incredible friendships I made by going to school in Tennessee.

Or the perfect setup I had for my four years of teaching.

Or the incredible community I have found in my church.

Or the freedom I have been able to enjoy in this season of singleness.

When I hear about "His higher ways and thoughts" I think of the gifts.

I don't often think of the challenges.

Think about it...the Scripture doesn't say His ways and thoughts will lead us to a place of comfort and perpetual happiness. It simply says He knows better than us.

What does that really mean? It means that those challenging seasons, tough decisions, and seemingly impossible moments are part of His ways and thoughts.

We would never write those into our future if it was up to us. Our plans and desires for ourselves only include the good, easy, and joyous moments. And yet, who we truly are and the way we live, most often come from the moments we would choose to avoid.

Our most life-defining moments are the ones we wouldn't have written into our story.

But He writes them in.

Our Father, in His good and perfect ways, knows the moments we avoid are the moments we can't live without.

Because it's in these moments – the ones where we find ourselves on our knees crying out for His help – we are reminded we are nothing without our Creator.

The diagnosis. The accident. The broken relationship. The lost job. The scary move. The hard decision. The season of waiting.

Those moments hold power.

OUR MOST LIFE-DEFINING MOMENTS ARE
THE ONES WE WOULDN'T HAVE
WRITTEN INTO OUR STORY.

So, in Isaiah 55, God isn't just referring to the blessings and added joy He is going to put in our lives, He is also referring to the hard moments – the ones we wish we could avoid.

In those moments – the ones that feel impossible and unbearable – we can know there is intention and thought and purpose behind it all.

So now, I look at life's worst and best moments through the lens of Isaiah 55.

The passing of my grandpa still stings. And when I let myself feel, it's an unbearable pit of sadness and loss I will never be able to find reason for. No one would have ever chosen cancer for Fuzzy or decided his life should have ended so soon, BUT our Creator numbers our days here on Earth, and His plans for Fuzzy were designed to bring him home at that specific moment.

Maliyah was born into a hurting family, BUT in His ways, our Father perfectly placed her in our family where we have found the completion and wholeness only He knew was possible. Her future is one of endless possibility and hope because of His protection and goodness in her life.

I vowed I wouldn't go to a college that was more than forty-five minutes away from home. God laughed and then I went to Tennessee because God told me to. The sadness I felt being so far from home and my family for three years was exhausting. The discomfort I experienced being somewhere I didn't totally want to be was hard, BUT in that time, I experienced some of my favorite moments and was gifted with some of my favorite friendships.

Our human lens is cracked, foggy, and zoomed in. Over time our life experiences, worldly influences, and human emotions have all damaged our lens. Each bad experience added another scratch and each hurtful word said to us made another dent. Ultimately, when we look at life through our own lens, we end up confused and frustrated.

But when we choose to look at life through an Isaiah 55 lens, we experience clarity. We get to see the vastness of the landscape. While we can't see all the details, we see the big picture – a life that is perfectly crafted to bring His name honor and glory.

————

OUR FATHER KNOWS THE MOMENTS
WE AVOID ARE THE MOMENTS
WE CAN'T LIVE WITHOUT.

————

Is it time to switch out your lens?

What moment are you in you wish you could avoid?

His perfection is all over it.

His hand is in every detail and is holding you up.

His ways are truly higher than your ways.

And how can I be so sure of that? Because my life is living proof of it.

The plan I had for my life was pretty spectacular – or so I thought it was.

By now you know that my childhood obsession was planning my perfect future and my adult obsession was trying to pull it off. You also know that my life as it stands is absolutely nothing like I had ever envisioned.

By 25 I should have been married, teaching, and looking to have a baby soon.

It makes me laugh to even type that last sentence. Oh, how little I know…

Instead, I am working at a church I love, finding a rhythm of rest I never thought was possible, investing in some really special relationships, leading worship, and getting to dive into the creative world in a way I had never imagined.

IT'S WILD.

When I was fifteen and singing with our youth worship band, a dear family friend was watching and listening and later told me God gave her a vision of me leading others in worship in the future. She had no idea the impact that would have on me.

For years I secretly clung to that statement. I told no one about it but always thought, "Well maybe in another lifetime I could be a worship leader because that definitely isn't in the cards for me." And then slowly over the last few years He has continued to open doors that have led to fulfillment of that dream – one that I never knew was even a possibility.

It was a far-off dream of mine to write a book, and yet, here I am.

I never would have planned these opportunities into my future because I didn't even know they were an option for me.

Did you catch that?

When we surrender to His ways, they will include things for us we didn't even know were an option.

We look at our life with our zoomed in lens and miss so much of what's even possible, but He looks at our life in its entirety and dreams up something spectacular for us.

The life He wants to give us, is one we didn't even know was a possibility because it's that good.

I feel like I'm finally living in this space where I can truly understand that His plans for me are better than my own...but it took me surrendering it all to get here.

I had to hold out my hands wide open, let go of control, and decide to walk in daily obedience.

Focused on Him...leaning in to hear His voice...making space for Him to move.

With Him, the seemingly impossible dreams become realities.

What seemingly impossible dream are you secretly harboring?

Are there things He has called you to that you are hesitant to believe because they seem unrealistic?

Surrender those dreams to Him. Stop clinging to them and instead, lay them down at His feet. Ask Him to lead you and show you what next step to take. Ask Him to bless what He wants to bless and rid you of whatever hinders you from walking the path of obedience.

If it's His will, He will make a way.

• • •

I'm discovering when you lay your plans down at His feet and walk in obedience to the path He has called you to take, you often find yourself in situations a bit outside your comfort zone.

He leads us to places we wouldn't go on our own.

> *"... 'My grace is sufficient for you, for my power is made perfect in weakness.' Therefore I will boast all the more gladly about my weaknesses, so that Christ's power may rest on me. That is why, for Christ's sake, I delight in weaknesses, in insults, in hardships, in persecutions, in difficulties. For when I am weak, then I am strong."*

2 Corinthians 12:9-10

Outside of our comfort zone – in moments of vulnerability – in unknown territory – we are desperate for and relying on His power, guidance, and strength. We are forced to lean on Him and turn to Him for our every need.

This is exactly where we want to be.

Desperate for Him and empowered by Him.

Every week as I get on stage to lead worship I utter this prayer, "Father, give me the boldness to remember You have called me, but the humility to remember You are equipping me."

In order to live a life that honors and serves Him, we must be humbled and recognize that without Him, we are nothing. He is the giver of all things.

To be fruitful and spread the Gospel, we must also recognize the power we are filled with – His power to carry out the tasks He has set before us.

A surrendered life is a beautiful contrast – it's one of humility and boldness.

In our weakest moments, He empowers us.

In our most vulnerable and broken form, we are His greatest weapons.

I've been talking about this weakness a lot with a friend of mine. This weakness that creates a gaping hole in your life, but when surrendered to our Father, will suddenly be filled with His power, direction, and goodness.

I have the honor of getting to sit with people and hear their stories. While my first role is to be there and listen, I often am also called to speak encouragement and truth into their lives and situations. Somehow, I'm supposed to have wisdom to offer, light to shed on the turmoil going on around them, and advice on what to do even if I have never experienced something similar.

And pretty much every time I find myself in this situation, I pray, "Father, give me Your words and Your wisdom. I'm Your vessel."

So often, the questions people ask are ones I'm still wrestling with myself. Their doubts are ones I carry, too. Their fears are the same ones I'm trying to fight.

I sit across from people who are broken, full of questions and doubts, fighting for the peace He promises us…and in my mind this makes me ill-equipped. But, in His mind, it makes me the perfect vessel.

He never said He would call the equipped. Instead, He promises to equip the called.

You see when I sit there, lacking the right words, He fills the space. When invited in, He comes and provides.

The words, the wisdom, the grace, the love…

When He asks you to witness to someone you know isn't a follower of Jesus, He will give you the words they are ready to hear.

When He tells you to stand up for something you believe in, He will give you the courage.

When someone in your life is going through a tough season and they need your support, He will show you what they need.

When He calls you, He will equip you, no matter what. He will not leave you lacking.

I used to pride myself on having it all together – my schedule, my emotions, my plan, my faith – there were no holes in my life. I made no space for gaps. If one began to form, I filled it with something.

Gaps made me feel vulnerable and out of control. They made me feel weak and susceptible to meltdowns. They created space for reflection and growth. All of those things made me uncomfortable.

All I wanted was stability and predictability for my life.

But, as you have seen over these last nine chapters, I have lost all that.

I have massive gaps in my life.

When is my husband coming my way? Will I ever go back to teaching? What does my future in ministry look like? Will He provide for me financially?

What gaps do you have in your life?

These gaps, while I often wish I could fill them, have done the perfect thing – taken away any stability and predictability I was creating on my own, and instead they have forced me to seek stability and predictability in the only One Who is those things.

My plan feels unstable and unpredictable.

My emotions feel unstable and unpredictable.

And honestly, in the best way possible, my faith feels unstable and unpredictable.

When I stand on stage Sunday mornings hoping to lead people in worship, I look to Him.

When I talk with a friend who is struggling to feel God and I'm trying to encourage them, I look to Him.

When I begin to feel the weight of life, I look to Him.

Moses did the same thing.

In Exodus 3 after encountering God in a burning bush, he asks the greatest question: ***"Who am I** that I should go to Pharaoh and bring the Israelites out of Egypt?"*

And God's response is the best! ***"I will be with you."***

215

Later, after God gives him clear direction on how this whole thing is going to go, Moses is still thinking God's got the wrong guy.

> *"Moses said to the Lord, 'Pardon your servant, Lord. I have never been eloquent, neither in the past nor since you have spoken to your servant. I am slow of speech and tongue.'*
>
> *The Lord said to him, 'Who gave human beings their mouths? Who makes them deaf or mute? Who gives them sight or makes them blind? Is it not I, the Lord? Now go;* **I will help you** *speak and* **will teach you** *what to say.'*
>
> *But Moses said, 'Pardon your servant, Lord. Please send someone else.'"*

Exodus 4:10-13 (emphasis added)

Sometimes the Bible can be hard to relate to, but Moses? I feel his pain.

God, are you talking to me? Really? I think you've got the wrong person.

- I'm not talented enough.
- I didn't go to school for that.
- I am new to this whole faith thing.
- I've messed up way too many times.
- I am not a people person.
- I don't like confrontation.
- I haven't read enough of the Bible.
- I come from a broken family.
- I'm divorced.
- I don't have extra time.
- That's not my thing.

- I've been to prison.
- I'm not very good at that.

God, I don't think you want to use me.

And do you know what He whispers?

"My child, I really do want to use you. Broken, doubting, and weary because when you are weak, then I am strong. Where you are lacking, I provide. Where you see barriers, I see opportunity to move mountains. I will provide all you need. I will equip you to do My work. You simply need to say yes."

His plans are better than yours.

In His plans, your brokenness is beautiful. Your trials are opportunities. Your weakness is made strong.

His plan for your life is far beyond what you could imagine or dream up. It will include moments on mountain tops – where the blessings are raining down and you can't stop smiling. It will also include moments in the darkest valleys – where the pain and hurt keeps coming and the tears won't stop flowing.

Yet somehow, in His perfect ways, it will all work out to create something beautiful.

> *"And we know that in all things God works for the good of those who love him, who have been called according to his purpose."*
>
> Romans 8:28

You are not too broken.

You are not lacking talent.

You are not without purpose.

You have been CALLED.

Called to love. Called to speak truth. Called to offer hope. Called to give grace. Called to be a Kingdom builder.

Wherever you are today, right at this moment, He wants to use YOU.

He is here right now saying, "Go, I have called you. Surrender it all to Me."

• • •

Recently, so many of my friends have felt God lay it on their heart to do something they hadn't planned to do – pick up and move somewhere completely random, go back to school for a graduate degree, give their car away to someone who needed it, step back from something they love for a season of rest, write a book, start a new career…and honestly, it's been incredibly fun to sit on the sidelines and watch these moments unfold.

To pray with them as they seek wisdom, guidance, and direction on something they weren't planning on. And then because of His calling and their obedience, I get to sit and watch His hand lay it all out in front of them…slowly unfolding and revealing His many blessings for this new chapter.

Our Father called them, and they said yes.

And you know what's crazy? For most of them, the next step He called them to take didn't make much sense. It was something they weren't prepared for and didn't line up with the world's way of living.

Yet, as soon as they said yes to it, He opened doors left and right to lead the way.

Watching Him work in their hearts and watching the joy and peace they experience from surrender and obedience is remarkable.

Doing life with people like this grows my faith.

Here's what I've decided: I want to surround myself with people who will live recklessly for His name and His Kingdom.

Because I too, want to live recklessly for His name and His Kingdom.

When you think of the people in the Bible who did big things for His name, it often didn't make much sense and was foolish in the world's eyes.

Noah gave his time and energy to building an ark when it had never rained. Shadrach, Meshach, and Abednego continued to worship their King even if it meant being thrown in the fiery furnace. Moses spoke up against Pharaoh and demanded he let the Israelites go. Esther boldly approached the king to save the Jews. Joseph stayed faithful to Mary even when her pregnancy didn't make sense. The disciples abandoned their livelihood and even left their families to follow Jesus.

He asks us to live with this reckless abandon for the Kingdom.

"Then Jesus told his disciples, 'If anyone would come after me, let him deny himself and take up his cross and follow me.'"

Matthew 16:24 (ESV)

Deny ourselves the pleasure of comfort. Of stability and predictability. Of ease.

Deny ourselves our plans and choose His instead.

And when we do that, when we follow Him, peace and joy abound, and the fruit of our labor is plentiful.

Because of recklessly following God, Noah saved humanity. Shadrach, Meshach, and Abednego brought people to Jesus. Moses freed the Israelites. Esther saved the Jews.

Joseph and Mary raised our Savior. The disciples continued the ministry of Jesus and spread hope and truth to the whole world.

One of my favorite parts about the stories of my friends' reckless pursuit of Jesus, is that for most of them, the calling He gave them came in the form of a whisper.

There was no burning bush. There was no angel that appeared.

There was just a quiet whisper – a gut feeling – a gentle nudge – (hint hint: The Holy Spirit) – something that could have easily been ignored.

Here's another thing I've learned about following Jesus: if we want to follow Him, we have to listen closely.

As I mentioned earlier, I have had a handful of moments where God spoke with such clarity to me that it would have been hard to miss.

However, most times in life, He has spoken to me in quiet whispers.

As one of my pastors said, "God is always speaking, we just have to get in a position to listen."

And then when He calls us with a whisper, we have to be brave enough to act on it.

Faith is following that whisper even when it doesn't make sense.

I think back to my whisper from God on January 6, 2020, when I wrote the prayer, "Father, I feel you calling me to ministry."

It was nothing more than a gentle nudge, and had I ignored it, I would have missed so much of what He had in store for me. What He told me didn't make sense – I was good at my job and loved everything about it – but that didn't matter. He had completed that season of training me for the next position He'd prepared me for.

God isn't in the business of writing stories that make sense. He's in the business of writing stories that bring freedom, hope, healing, and redemption.

What kind of story are you living in?

He's looking for followers who will live with reckless abandon and with a whisper of His voice, go and do the work He has called them to do.

———

GOD ISN'T IN THE BUSINESS OF WRITING STORIES THAT MAKE SENSE. HE'S IN THE BUSINESS OF WRITING STORIES THAT BRING FREEDOM, HOPE, HEALING, AND REDEMPTION.

———

He isn't looking for perfect people.

He is looking for willing people.

He is looking for people with gaps He can fill.

He is looking for people who are attentive to His gentle whisper.

He is looking for people willing to surrender it all.

His ways are higher than our ways.

His thoughts are higher than our thoughts.

His heart is good, and His plans are perfect.

He desires to use YOU. He is calling YOU. Just as you are.

FAITH IS FOLLOWING THAT
WHISPER EVEN WHEN IT
DOESN'T MAKE SENSE.

Take a Minute

Remember

- Our most life-defining moments are the ones we wouldn't have written into our story.
- Our Father knows the moments we avoid are the moments we can't live without.
- With Him, the seemingly impossible dreams become realities.
- He never said He would call the equipped. Instead, He promises to equip the called.
- He asks us to live with reckless abandon for the Kingdom.
- Faith is following that whisper even when it doesn't make sense.
- God isn't in the business of writing stories that make sense. He's in the business of writing stories that bring freedom, hope, healing, and redemption.

Recite

"'I don't think the way you think. The way you work isn't the way I work.' GOD's Decree. 'For as the sky soars high above earth, so the way I work surpasses the way you work, and the way I think is beyond the way you think. Just as rain and snow descend from the skies and don't go back until they've watered the earth, Doing their work of making things grow and blossom, producing seed for farmers and food for the hungry, So will the words that come out of my mouth not come back empty-handed. They'll do the work I sent them to do, they'll complete the assignment I gave them.'"

Isaiah 55:8-11 (The Message) (emphasis added)

*"For my thoughts are not your thoughts, neither are your ways my ways,'
declares the LORD. 'As the heavens are higher than the earth, so are
my ways higher than your ways and my thoughts than your thoughts.'"*

Isaiah 55:8-9

*"... 'My grace is sufficient for you, for my power is made perfect in
weakness.' Therefore I will boast all the more gladly about my
weaknesses, so that Christ's power may rest on me. That is why, for
Christ's sake, I delight in weaknesses, in insults, in hardships, in
persecutions, in difficulties. For when I am weak, then I am strong."*

2 Corinthians 12:9-10

*"But Moses said to God, 'Who am I that I should go to Pharaoh and
bring the Israelites out of Egypt?'*

And God said, 'I will be with you.'"

Exodus 3:11-12

*"Moses said to the Lord, 'Pardon your servant, Lord. I have never been
eloquent, neither in the past nor since you have spoken to your servant. I
am slow of speech and tongue.'*

*The Lord said to him, 'Who gave human beings their mouths? Who
makes them deaf or mute? Who gives them sight or makes them blind?
Is it not I, the Lord? Now go;* **I will help you** *speak and* **will
teach you** *what to say.'*

But Moses said, 'Pardon your servant, Lord. Please send someone else.'"

Exodus 4:10-13

"And we know that in all things God works for the good of those who love him, who have been called according to his purpose."

Romans 8:28

"Then Jesus told his disciples, 'If anyone would come after me, let him deny himself and take up his cross and follow me.'"

Matthew 16:24 (ESV)

Reflect

- Are you in a moment you wish you could avoid?
- Looking back, is there a moment you wouldn't have written into your story but now you can see His hand all over it?
- What good things has He blessed you with that you didn't even know were an option for you?
- What seemingly impossible dream are you secretly harboring? Are there things He has called you to that you are hesitant to believe because they seem unrealistic?
- What people in your life live with reckless abandon for His Kingdom?
- How has He called you?

Respond

Take a few minutes to talk with God about what is stirring in your heart. Thank Him for the perfect story He has written for you. Thank Him for the things He has put in your life you didn't even know were an option for you. If you are currently in a situation you wish you could avoid, ask Him to reveal His presence and plan to you. Surrender everything to Him including those dreams that feel impossible. Ask Him to lead you and show you what next step to take. Ask Him to bless what He wants to bless and rid you of whatever hinders you from walking the path of obedience. Quiet your mind and make space to hear His gentle whispers.

Chapter ten

the power of one

the power of one

What I want to share with you in this chapter is so vitally important. If we, as disciples of Jesus, need to remember one thing it is this…there is so much power in one.

One person. One heart. One salvation.

The story I am about to share with you is ALL about our good Father and the salvation of His children.

The story reminds us how important it is to take action when He calls us. To be obedient to His voice. To surrender to His Kingdom building.

This is one of my favorite, "because God told me to," moments.

I had a friend named Lisa, and Lisa changed my life forever.

Four and a half years ago she walked into the school where I was teaching as our new reading recovery teacher. About six months later, she was diagnosed with her second form of cancer. The prognosis was not good, and it was clear she was going to have to fight hard.

Our staff began to figure out ways we could rally around her and as they began to donate money for wigs and sign up to provide meals, God told me something different. He told me I needed to go buy her the book *Jesus Calling* and write her a card that pointed her towards Him.

I was hesitant because I barely knew her at the time. I didn't want to be THAT person who shoved Jesus down her throat. But I knew what He was asking me to do and I wanted to be obedient.

I bought the pink leather version of the book, put it in a cute gift bag, wrote a card, and one morning before she was in the building, I stuck it on her desk and ran to my classroom. I was nervous about how the gift would be received. After all, I had no idea what she believed when it came to Jesus.

Later, she graciously thanked me for the gift, and it was at that moment God made something so clear to me – I was to fervently pursue her heart until she discovered how loved she was by her Creator.

Suddenly, she became my one.

Over the next three years, she got calls that told her she was cancer free and then received news the cancer was everywhere. Physically and emotionally, she was on a roller coaster. There was no consistency or stability to any of it.

As I walked alongside her, I did my best to show her Who Jesus was. I invited her to church (over and over and over) to the point where I assumed she was very tired of me asking. I sent her sermons to listen to, Bible verses to read, devotions I thought she would find encouraging, and worship songs I thought she would like.

And along with these things, I prayed and prayed and prayed. I prayed for her health but most importantly her heart.

On January 3, 2020, I wrote this prayer,

"Father, Lisa's cancer is back. I'm so broken. I hate seeing her fight this disease again and again, but even more I hate seeing her fight without knowing You. I wish she would surrender everything to You. Show me how I can keep loving her."

In July of that year my pastor delivered a sermon about the story of the lost sheep found in the opening verses of Luke 15.

> *"Suppose one of you has a hundred sheep and loses one of them. Doesn't he leave the ninety-nine in the open country and go after the lost sheep until he finds it? And when he finds it, he joyfully puts it on his shoulders and goes home. Then he calls his friends and neighbors together and says, 'Rejoice with me; I have found my lost sheep.' I tell you that in the same way there will be more rejoicing in heaven over one sinner who repents than over ninety-nine righteous persons who do not need to repent."*

The sermon went on to talk about the importance of followers of Jesus chasing after that one person God has laid on their heart.

I sent this sermon to Lisa and after listening, Lisa texted me asking, "Am I your one?"

I told her yes. She was my one. That ever since she had walked into the doors of my school, God had laid it on my heart to pursue her.

Her text back said, "Any small/beginner steps I could take to begin my relationship? In my opinion, if YOU love it, it's GOT to be good."

For the next eight months Lisa dove in. She began reading the Bible and sending me questions over things she didn't understand. She began watching church online and was able to come to an in-person service. Our favorite thing was to send worship songs back and forth to one another.

And then it happened. On December 10, 2020, she wrote a Facebook status sharing with everyone that she had found a relationship with Jesus.

It was one of the sweetest days of my life.

Three months later, she found herself back in the hospital with the news of tumors in her stomach and colon. Everyone expected her to be released, but on a Wednesday evening I got a phone call from a dear friend that the doctors found tumors in her brain, and they didn't know if she would make it through the weekend.

I got off the phone and crumbled. I was devastated. I wasn't ready for this.

I knew I needed to go see her the next day. Knowing friends and family would be saying their goodbyes, I wanted to go early. Visiting hours started at six in the morning and something in my spirit told me to show up as soon as I could.

Before I went to bed that night, I got on my knees, opened my Bible to Psalm 23, and sobbed. I was so worried about her heart and how she was feeling. Was she scared or at peace? Did she need to be reminded God was with her and He was holding her? I needed to go sing with her, pray with her, and remind her it was all going to be okay.

"God, I don't know how to do this. I don't know what to say to her. I am not ready for this."

I was so uneasy at the idea of guiding someone's heart in their final moments, but I knew He was calling me to go.

I prayed He would lead me.

The next morning, I found myself walking through the hospital doors before the sun was up. The hospital was quiet, and I took a seat next to Lisa. She was unresponsive and had taken a turn for the worse during the night. I wasn't sure what to do, so I did the one thing I knew how to do – I sang.

I sang some of her favorite worship songs, I prayed over her, and I read Scripture. I prayed that no matter what happened in that hospital room over the next twenty-four hours, His presence would fill the space and His peace would be felt by everyone.

Eventually Lisa's mom and sister walked into the room. I had only met her mom once and assuming they didn't know who I was, I introduced myself. To my surprise, they knew exactly who I was. I was known as Lisa's "Jesus friend."

After talking with them, to honor their family and time with Lisa, I thought it was best to leave. I hugged them all and told them I was praying and here for whatever they needed.

As I walked out of the hospital, I got a call from my friend who had given me the news that previous evening. She told me she was going to come and sit in the waiting room. I asked if she wanted a friend to sit with her, and when she said yes, I turned back around and cancelled my plans for the day.

For the next fourteen hours family and friends came and went, all saying their final goodbyes. There were many moments where I almost left, exhausted from the day and wanting to be sure I wasn't imposing on the family, but each time I almost left, something in me told me to stay.

I was able to have conversations with Lisa's sisters about the faith Lisa had found in the last year. We all celebrated what an answer to prayer it was. Lisa's family had been praying for her salvation for a long time.

That evening around eight o'clock, hospice came and took Lisa off her support. They told us that once they removed the support, she could pass in a matter of minutes or hours. It was impossible to know. We gathered in the hospital room, and readied ourselves for this final goodbye.

About twenty minutes in, my friend suggested I sing, and when the family agreed they liked that idea, we all began to lift our voices and praise His name.

We sang a few of Lisa's favorite songs like *O Come All Ye Faithful* and declared His goodness with songs like *Great Is Thy Faithfulness*. While Lisa's body slowly began to stop fighting, everyone's voice filled the room with praise.

At one point, one of her sisters said, "I feel so at peace right now. This room feels so good and so full of love."

An answer to prayer.

My prayer the whole day was that His presence would fill the room and His peace would be felt by everyone.

Around nine thirty, someone requested I sing *In Christ Alone*. Everyone was surrounding Lisa and suddenly, as we began to sing, her vitals started to drop. On the last line of the second verse as we sang, "Here in the death of Christ I live," Lisa let go.

It was a moment you would see in a movie. Perfectly written by the Author of our lives.

Lisa let go of this side of heaven surrounded by those she loved most who were lifting up the One who was in control of it all.

And just like that, she was free of pain, sorrow, and cancer – and in the sweetest and most beautiful of ways – she met her Savior and found rest in His arms.

As people were hugging one another and breathing a sigh of relief, I felt God whisper to me, "Pray."

Not wanting to interrupt the moment but trying to be obedient to His voice that had carried me through the day, I asked the family if I could pray.

All I could think was, "I got to walk alongside my friend as she found Jesus, and today I got to sing alongside her as she ran into the arms of her Savior."

What a gift.

I left the hospital, climbed in my car, and let the tears come.

They came for days.

I knew where Lisa was. I knew there was joy in that. But, I was really sad.

I had been so excited to walk alongside Lisa as she experienced Jesus on this side of heaven. We had talked about baptism. I was excited for her to come to church events. I wanted her to share her story with those around her. I wanted to continue seeing the smile on her face as she experienced the freedom that came with knowing and trusting Jesus. I wanted to do it all with her.

Instead, it was her time to go meet her Savior face to face.

This is way better for her, but I feel like I am missing out. My sweet Lisa, who I'm so incredibly proud of, is healed and whole.

As I write this chapter, it's a few weeks later and I'm still processing it all. Lisa's life impacted me in more ways than I can express.

Because Lisa isn't here to share her story, I've written this vital piece of it and I know it will transform the lives of those who read this book and so many others who hear it repeated.

I have found clarity on a few things I learned through my friendship with Lisa and I feel compelled to share them with you, so here's what I want you to know...

God is pursuing you.

The week between Lisa's passing and her funeral, I had the privilege of talking to many of her friends and family. One person after another told me how much they had been praying for Lisa to find Jesus. For her whole life, Lisa had been covered in prayer by those who knew and loved her in hopes she would find the eternal life, hope, and healing found in Him.

God placed people in Lisa's path with such loving intention and perfection. He never left her side. He was with her through every tragedy, heartbreak, and joy she experienced throughout her life. And most importantly, He was there in her final moments, in that hospital room; then was waiting with open arms as she was able to run freely into them.

None of Lisa's story caught Him by surprise – not the diagnosis of cancer, not the return of it, and definitely not the day Lisa took her last breath. God had been in pursuit of Lisa's heart from the day He created her, and He knew the day she would get to meet Him face to face.

In the same way God pursued Lisa, He is pursuing you.

Her story reminds us that we are never alone, never forgotten, and never without hope. We don't walk through any of life by ourselves. At any moment we can choose to turn to our Father, Who is walking right alongside us, guiding us, protecting us, and loving us.

One of my favorite texts I got from Lisa was back in January after she had gotten some discouraging news about her health and she said, "I'm kinda freaking out right now. Not as bad as I would be feeling had I not found the Lord." That right there…that is hope.

In the midst of fear, doubt, and pain, Lisa had found the One to cling to – the One Who is steadfast, constant, always there, and never far away.

She was able to end her fight knowing she was held by her Creator, loved dearly, and had nothing to fear.

God had His hand all over Lisa's life from the time He created her. He pursued Lisa's heart and He's also pursuing yours.

Surrender is made up of big moments of obedience and lots of little moments of obedience.

If you look back through the chapters in this book, you'll find confirmation of the power of surrendering to God in big moments. Things like a career change, buying a house, or writing a book. But looking back on what I learned most recently, surrendering your life to God doesn't just include being obedient with the big decisions.

It also includes these small consistent moments of immediate obedience.

When I look back on that Thursday at the hospital, I am so grateful I kept saying yes to His subtle guidance.

"Morgan, go to the hospital right when visiting hours start."

"Morgan, stay at the hospital with your friend."

"Morgan, stay until the end."

"Morgan, sing and praise My name."

"Morgan, pray with the family."

His whispers were subtle and I didn't have time to sit and pray on it. Instead, I had to trust His voice and just say yes.

Every single day we are challenged with moments of immediate obedience.

At the grocery store we might feel the urge to ask the cashier how they are doing.

We might feel prompted to call someone and ask how we can pray for them.

Maybe you are talking with a neighbor and God encourages you to invite them to church.

He might ask you to get on your knees or raise your hands during worship.

Maybe you feel Him ask you to give twenty dollars to the person standing on the street corner.

Whatever it is, it's those little moments where He clearly tells you what to do and your insides flip inside out because you are terrified to be obedient.

But in those moments, there is no time to debate. The window of opportunity is small and if you don't act instantly, you miss the moment.

There's no time for analyzing your own fear, just enough time to act on His guidance.

This sort of obedience requires us to be in tune with Him. In step and in sync with His heart and His desire for His people. Always asking Him to speak to us.

It means we must be in His Word consistently, prayerful each and every day, and always seeking to be refined to look more like Him.

Don't let these small moments of immediate obedience pass you by. They matter.

There is never a wrong moment to praise.

I never stop singing. I joke all the time about it, and it drives my siblings crazy, but it truly is what I feel most natural and comfortable doing. There is always a song in my head.

When I got to Lisa's room that morning, the hospital was eerily quiet, and the sound of the monitors and machines were unsettling. Honestly, I felt really uncomfortable, and was unsure of what to do…so I did the one thing I knew to do that always brought me peace – praise.

Later that day as I sat in the room with Lisa's mom and friend, it was uncomfortably quiet as the sadness and pain from the day hung like a heavy fog, so I sang. And they joined in. Song after song we lifted up His name and praised Him for His goodness. The heavy fog lifted, and a spirit of peace filled the room.

Then, that evening, as everyone was standing around Lisa in her final hour, we praised. With medical masks covering our faces, exhausted bodies, and tearful sobs, we lifted our voices to the only One who heals. To the One who created Lisa, pursued Lisa, and was now ready to welcome her home.

It was one of those moments – a series of small moments – that I'll never be able to fully describe, but will never ever forget. His Spirit fell on that room in a way I have never experienced before. Jesus came and wrapped His arms around each and every person in that room and everyone felt His embrace.

In each of these moments, there was a part of me thinking, "This is so awkward…" but then I would think about Lisa and her story. Worship music was the thing that broke her walls down enough to think about letting Jesus in. Worship music helped her feel Him in a way she had never felt Him before. So what if I felt awkward? Praising His name brought her peace, and in her final moments, that's all I wanted for her and everyone else in that room.

I walked away that night realizing that there is never a wrong moment to praise. No matter how awkward. No matter how it sounds. No matter what people think. He is always deserving of our worship and when we praise His name, His presence is felt.

When we praise Him, we invite Him into that space in such a beautiful way. We purposefully soften our hearts to feel Him and in doing so, we provide those around us with the opportunity to experience Him, too.

His song can fill our hearts all day long.

"Praise the LORD. How good it is to sing praises to our God, how pleasant and fitting to praise him!"

Psalm 147:1

Pursue your one.

When I look back on my time with Lisa, I am awestruck by the gift my Father gave me. There were so many people praying for her and guiding her heart towards Jesus. I just so happened to be the one who got to watch it all unfold from the front row.

I mean it when I say that being a part of Lisa's story was one of the greatest privileges ever.

God could have picked anyone in Lisa's life to sit where I got to sit, but He gifted me with the opportunity.

While the cancer was fierce and we all were wondering how long her body could fight it, her final days caught us by surprise. We all thought she would have more time at home – and with us.

A few days after she passed away, one thought hit me – what if I wouldn't have pursued her as fervently as I did?

I know God is big enough to cover my shortcomings. The fruition of His plans and the hearts of His people don't rest on my shoulders. But had I not been obedient to His calling on my life to pursue Lisa, only He knows what the outcome would have been.

I sure would not have been a part of her story in such a special way.

We don't know how long anyone has here on Earth, which means we can't waste time.

We all have someone God has laid on our heart to pursue. (If you don't think you do, ask Him. He will show you.)

Stop sitting around and waiting for the right moment.

Stop waiting for it to feel right or easy or comfortable.

A conversation about someone's eternity shouldn't necessarily be comfortable, it should be urgent.

And let me take the stress away and remind you that it is not up to you to save someone, it is just up to you to offer them a chance to learn about the One who saves.

I am so grateful I didn't waste time with Lisa, but who have I wasted time with?

Who have you wasted time with?

Who is your one and what do you need to do to pursue them?

Take a Minute

Remember

- God is pursuing you.
- Surrender is made up of big moments of obedience and lots of little moments of immediate obedience.
- There's never a wrong moment to praise.
- His song can fill our hearts all day long.
- Pursue your one.
- A conversation about someone's eternity shouldn't necessarily be comfortable, it should be urgent.

Recite

"Suppose one of you has a hundred sheep and loses one of them. Doesn't he leave the ninety-nine in the open country and go after the lost sheep until he finds it? And when he finds it, he joyfully puts it on his shoulders and goes home. Then he calls his friends and neighbors together and says, 'Rejoice with me; I have found my lost sheep.' I tell you that in the same way there will be more rejoicing in heaven over one sinner who repents than over ninety-nine righteous persons who do not need to repent."

Luke 15:4-7

"Praise the LORD. How good it is to sing praises to our God, how pleasant and fitting to praise him!"

Psalm 147:1

Reflect

- Do you believe God is pursuing you? If so, what ways have you seen Him pursue you?
- When God urges you to do something, are you quick to obey? Is immediate obedience something that is easy or hard for you?
- How often do you praise Him?
- Who is your one? What steps do you know you are supposed to take to pursue them?

Respond

Take a few minutes to talk with God about what is stirring in your heart. Who is your one? Take the next few minutes praying for that person. If you don't have someone in mind, ask God to show you who that person might be. Pray for their heart and that it would be softened to know and accept Jesus. Ask God to give you His wisdom and discernment. Ask Him what next step you might take in order to pursue them. Ask Him to use you and speak to you. Finally, ask Him to give you the boldness to be obedient to His voice and direction.

Chapter eleven

*what's your story going
to be made up of?*

what's your story going to be made up of?

When I taught second grade, writing time was one of my favorite parts of the day. Giving kids space for their imaginations to come to life and encouraging them to try and use words to put their thoughts on paper was so fun. They never failed to write things that made me smile. But, I found the most difficult concept to teach in writing was how to write a good conclusion. I always referred to the conclusion as "the bow." I'd say, "Just as you would tie a beautiful bow around a present to wrap it up, the purpose of your conclusion is to wrap up your thoughts in the best way possible."

I taught them that whatever was in their conclusion was what they were going to leave their reader thinking about. The conclusion determined how their reader was going to be left feeling.

It was their last chance to leave an impact on their reader.

So, with that in mind, I've wondered how I was going to tie a bow on the 55,000 words in this book.

What lasting thought and feeling do I want to leave you with?

• • •

The book of John captures much of Jesus' time here on earth as it details accounts of miracles He performed, sermons He taught, and relationships He formed. It ends with the resurrection of Jesus and

His conversation with Peter where He leaves Peter with one lasting charge – feed My sheep and follow Me.

The last verse of the book of John is a perfect example of a beautiful conclusion.

"Jesus did many other things as well. If every one of them were written down, I suppose that even the whole world would not have room for the books that would be written."

John 21:25

The whole world could not contain the stories that tell of all He has done.

Let that sink in for a minute.

The lives our Savior has touched, the miracles He has performed, the work He has done...it cannot be contained on paper. It is far too vast for that.

Our God cannot be simplified into words. He is far too great for that.

While we can't capture *everything* He has done, we can absolutely share what He has done in *our* lives.

Each of us has a story of our own – from our first breath to our last, each moment was written by our Father with intention, design, and perfection. Each story is unique – no two are the same. And each one has His handprint all over.

I used to believe I didn't have a testimony. Because I was raised in church, never strayed far from my relationship with Jesus, and can't tell you the exact date I gave my life to Him, I didn't believe there was much of a story to tell.

Others around me shared stories of previous drug addiction, abusive relationships, broken homes, or eating disorders. Their story of coming to know Jesus and finding forgiveness and freedom in Him seemed far more enticing and impactful than mine.

And because I believed that – for far too long – when asked to share a testimony, I said I didn't really have one, or that mine was too boring and not worth listening to.

I didn't think I had a story worth telling.

That is, until a few weeks ago when God brought everything full circle for me, and it hit me smack in the face – this book is my story.

I hadn't realized that over the last nine months, I had been writing my story – my testimony.

I finally began to understand that I do have a story – one that matters. One that shares a personal experience of the power, joy, and peace that comes from living a life of surrender.

My story tells of a girl who tried to achieve a standard of perfection in order to please the onlookers – but found freedom in embracing her imperfection.

My story tells of a girl who thought she needed to sprint through life in order to make it worthwhile – but discovered a life rooted in Him equated to rest because He is enough.

My story tells of a girl who met others with judgment and condemnation – but eventually came to understand the power of lavishing others in His grace.

My story tells of a lost daughter in a broken world – finding her way home into the arms of her loving Father.

My story is a testimony of the power that comes from complete surrender.

And the incredible truth is that through each person's story we hear, two things happen. First, we are given a chance to grow our grace, and second, our trust in our Father increases.

You see, it's easy to judge someone you don't know. It's much harder to judge someone who has shown you their heart. When we are given the opportunity to hear the story of another person, empathy comes rushing in. We are suddenly reminded that each one of us is broken and in desperate need of our Savior. Our worldview expands. We begin to better understand the why behind the behavior. Rather than judgment, we can offer understanding. Our grace grows.

And, as someone shares their story, because their experiences and feelings are different than ours, we gain the opportunity to expand our view of God - to see Him in a different light. To understand Him in a different way. To experience His character through the story of one of His children. We walk away knowing and trusting Him a bit more.

It's a beautiful thing. Our understanding of the Creator and Author of our lives grows each time we get a glimpse into a different story He has written.

Over the next few pages, you'll read several stories of surrender.

Each person and the part of their story they have chosen to share is so different, but He is consistent. God's character, faithfulness, and goodness is woven into every facet. His handiwork is in every detail.

As you read, I pray that you will delight in the work He has done in the lives of His children because they said yes to surrendering... and that your grace will grow as your understanding of Him expands.

• • •

In 2012, my husband and I were entering our fifth year of pastoral ministry at a church that we loved. We were both pastors on staff while also working other jobs and raising our first child. Our plates were very full, but we loved every last thing our lives held.

However, as we finished up a few weeks of fasting and praying for direction, we felt God asking us to step away from pastoral ministry for an entire year. He wanted us to take some time to rest and learn so that we could be ready for the next season He had for us.

We were absolutely shocked! Rest? That didn't seem right. We needed to go and do and build God's Kingdom. We wrestled with the instructions for quite some time, unsure what life would look like with more margin and, what we thought would be less purpose. God continued to press it on our hearts, though.

So, we obeyed. We walked away from the only lifestyle we had ever known as a married couple and took a year to simply be. We focused on our growing family, building relationships at my husband's company, our marriage, old friends that we hadn't caught up with in years. We focused on the act of obeying one of God's commands, "remember the Sabbath and keep it holy."

When we entered that season, I naively thought it was just a sacrifice I needed to make because God asked me to. I thought He wanted me to prove that I would follow His leading, that I could give up something that I had enjoyed, that I could push past people pleasing to obey. In short, I thought this season was meant to prove something to God when instead, it was actually to prove something to me.

God used that time to teach us our limits. We had never made rest, Sabbath, and balance a part of our family rhythm. We didn't know the value and the beauty of it. Sure, we knew how to obey and how to serve, but we didn't know when to stop, when to let our limits show and God's limitless power to take over.

That time was a gift.

God told us to do it not because He wanted us to suffer in letting go of something and sitting by in obscurity. No, His instructions refreshed us. They brought us peace and helped us build new habits. Habits of rest and balance.

Habits that served us well as we dove back in, slowly but surely, into different forms of ministry. The years since then have seen us plant a church and add more children to our family. They have seen my husband grow as a leader in both the Christian and corporate spheres. They have seen me grow as a writer and speaker. And they have seen us apply the wisdom God allowed us to find through that year of rest.

You see, He wanted us to grow in our capacity, so He taught us what that capacity actually was. We wouldn't have been ready for what God had for us, had we not obeyed what He asked to do.

We never would have found it on our own, but because God told us to, we discovered the gifts that were hidden on the other side of obedience.

~ Kelsey Lasher

• • •

In the summer of 2006, I found out I was pregnant with my third child. With mixed emotions we began to embrace the idea of a growing family. At around eight weeks pregnant I had the most vivid dream I had a baby girl. In the dream, she had this perfect circular birthmark in the center of her forehead. At the time it seemed weird, and I brushed it off as one of those pregnancy dreams.

Many weeks later I discovered I really was having a girl.

At 24 weeks I was admitted to the hospital on bedrest for the remainder of my pregnancy because of the possibility of the baby's "failure to thrive." I was very scared of having a premature baby and all the complications that go along with it. I prayed everyday she wouldn't come yet, especially after learning more about all the potential complications that can happen with preemies. I also knew I needed to name her sooner rather than later. My husband and I tossed around names, but nothing felt good enough. Then, it was laid upon my heart very strongly that her name should be a testament to our faith and her life. With that feeling, and also a sense of hope that God would give me a miracle, we named her Faith.

October 27 came too quickly and at 26 weeks my baby was born. I remember that day so clearly – hearing her cry and holding her for the first time. She was strong, her face was perfect in every way, and there was no beauty mark on her forehead. "Just a crazy dream," I thought. She was quickly moved to the NICU.

The next couple days merged together as I came to grips with what had happened and her devastating diagnosis of being born with Tetralogy of Fallot, a complicated heart defect that we were unaware of before birth. Over the next few weeks, I sat with her every day and experienced a roller coaster of emotions.

Then, one morning I got the call. On November 21 she was diagnosed with NEC (Necrotizing Enterocolitis) – a devastating intestinal disease common in premature babies. Later that morning she was airlifted to another hospital. Faith immediately went into surgery and survived. It was a very long night for all of us. The next day she was still not improving, and the doctors were losing hope. Everyone was praying and hoping for a miracle.

Her veins were collapsing and making it harder for the doctors to give her new IV's. The last IV they gave her was in the top of her head. When I saw her then, I knew. It all came back in an instant. I knew God was preparing me and was answering prayers.

That last IV had broken a small blood vessel in her head leaving a perfect round circle in the middle of her forehead. She was going home.

In that moment I knew that while I was praying for a miracle of healing, it was God's plan to take her home. He had prepared me for this day. I didn't fail my daughter. I didn't give up on her. She was a gift from God and that day – November 22, 2006 – I chose to give her back.

She may have lived a little longer on tubes and could have died at any moment alone in a hospital bed, but that evening we took all her tubes away and held her for the last time before she entered the arms of our loving God.

~ Andria Marsh

• • •

My name is Brady Wright, and I am the Lead Pastor of Fresh Hope Church in the Parker-Aurora area of Colorado. In 2015 I was at a church conference in Jacksonville, Florida serving the pastors and leaders who were there. I was in my second year of Bible College, and only three years removed from God delivering me from a heroin addiction.

During the last session of the conference, I managed to secure a seat for myself in the upper deck of a large mega-church auditorium. I really did not know what to expect that night, but something was telling me to go check it out. The message that night was about calling, and at the end there was an altar call. I did not go to the altar (like many did). I stayed in my seat waiting, anticipating God to reveal something to me in the moment.

What happened next drastically changed the direction of my life.

There have been two times in my life where I felt the Holy Spirit speak something into me that was so clear it could have been an audible voice. One was just after giving my heart to Jesus following years of addiction where God told me He was going to restore our family. If you knew us in that season, you would have known that it would have taken a miracle. However, God shares in Isaiah 55:8-9, *"Just as the Heavens are higher than the earth as are my ways your ways and my*

257

thoughts your thoughts." I pursued that dream, and here we are today with an incredible marriage, and four amazing kids.

The other time was this particular night in Jacksonville. God told me during this special moment, "I want you and Bridget (my wife) to one day pastor a local, life-giving church whose generosity and compassion touch the world."

Like any good dream God puts in your heart, this scared me to death! ME? How could I ever do something like that? I did not come from a long line of ministers, I was by far not the smartest person in my class, and I had only known Jesus for a couple years. Surely, I thought, God had the wrong guy!

It would have been easy for me to downplay the call, but I knew that God had spoken.

Over the next six years we prayed over that dream and watered it every opportunity that we got. We served, and we loved.

At the beginning of 2020, five years after the vision, God revealed to us that it was time.

Days before a global pandemic would begin, our Father told us it was time for His dream for our lives to become a reality. Therefore, we stepped out to plant Fresh Hope Church. After spending the next year building a team of people, and raising funds, we launched March 21, 2021.

As I am writing this, we are fourteen weeks old as a church and have seen over 300 people walk through our doors, 24 salvations, and 8 baptisms.

A friend of mine once said, "If your dream doesn't scare you, then it's not big enough."

When God places a dream in your heart, go for it. You just may catch a glimpse of Heaven in the process.

~Brady Wright

•••

"Only God can turn a mess into a message, a test into a testimony, a trial into a triumph, a victim into a victory." If that does not sum up our family, I don't know what does.

Two years into marriage, my husband and I merely wanted a child, a family. We were young, naïve, and hopeful for our future. Just a couple months into our process to adopt, we received the referral of a beautiful, healthy four-month-old baby boy. Just two months later we were on a plane to a small country 6,000 miles away to meet our son.

My heart was broken in a way I never thought possible when I saw the conditions these children were living in. The smells were overwhelming, and the eerie silence was deafening.

When they brought our son to us, we were shocked. We had been told he was four months old and healthy. This child in front of us was not healthy. He was one year old and weighed eleven pounds. He was emaciated, weak, pale, and sickly.

My initial feeling was to turn and run – I was terrified, but God kept us firmly planted in that space. He helped us survive the next fourteen days in a foreign country with a fragile baby who couldn't stand to be touched or fed and who screamed constantly. As I walked out of the orphanage with that sick, little boy, I knew we would return someday. The seeds were planted, our hearts and souls were shattered, and we were forever changed.

God worked on our hearts and called us to adopt again from the same orphanage except He called us to *request* a child with special needs. We were quickly matched with a little girl who had severe cleft lip and palate. Unfortunately, due to political instability, it would be six years before she came home and as funds dwindled and our hearts broke more and more each day, it became harder to stick with a process that seemed like it would never end with a child in our arms.

But God helped provide the funds, He provided the strength, and He provided the knowledge and resources we needed to continue to fight for her. Eventually she came home, but during those six years she suffered severe abuse and a brain injury.

During the six years we waited for her, we were led to adopt three other children.

Our first was a little girl who was born sixteen weeks premature and had severe medical issues. One day I received an email with a brief paragraph about a little girl followed with, "Are you still interested in adopting this child?" I have no clue how or why I received the email, but when I reached out, I received a response from a social worker.

She was, indeed, a real child looking for a real family.

Over the next several days I prayed and researched her needs. When I sat down to tell my husband about her, he said, "When do we go?"

Two weeks later, after a whirlwind of preparing for a fragile infant, we hopped on a plane to Louisiana. There is no earthly reason she should have made it into our life, but He knew we needed her.

One day, a friend shared a picture of a little girl in another country who was sick and in desperate need of a family. I can't explain why I made contact with that agency except that God led me to do it. The little girl had five families considering adopting her, so the agency asked if we would consider a same-age, same-diagnoses little boy that was in the same orphanage as her. We said yes.

Months later the agency told us that all the families considering adopting the little girl had backed out and we were welcome to "switch" our process back to adopting her. How in the world could we change our minds about this little boy that we had grown to love from afar? How in the world could we walk away from the little girl who had led us to this little boy?

So...we decided to adopt both children. A year after beginning the process, our two new children came home. Two years later, our daughter was finally freed from the orphanage that had held her hostage for six and a half years.

We were finally a family – complete.

God provided for and orchestrated every single adoption. He placed each child in front of us at just the right time and gave us the courage to move. I never planned to have a large family and I certainly never thought I was capable of parenting children with difficult diagnoses.

Amongst our five children, there are over thirty medical diagnoses. They have collectively survived over 120 surgeries, hundreds of days in the hospital and hundreds of procedures. I have stood, watched on and prayed silently through two full codes on our youngest daughter. I have shed more tears than I knew possible. I never would have believed I was equipped for any of it, but here I am. I have aged beyond my years. I have seen things that one hopes they never have to see. I have made impossible decisions, and comforted children who suffered unimaginably.

All of it has helped shape me into the person God always wanted me to be. It's easier for me now to trust Him, to give it all over to Him, to believe that no matter how hard things are, it's right where He wants me to be, and He will be by my side to carry me through it.

Our family is messy; it is hard; we have faced many trials and suffered many tragedies, and we have all emerged victorious.

~ Shannon Fenske

• • •

It was 2020 and all hell was breaking loose. Tornadoes destroyed our town, the pandemic forced us to isolate, and a whole series of life-altering events would follow. I began to struggle and crave connection, growth, and support, so I decided to be bold and do something God had laid on my heart long ago to do – ask this amazing woman of God at my church, Amy, to be my mentor. Despite my awkward request to this woman who I simply aspired to be more like, she said yes! We began meeting once a month, and in our first breakfast meeting she said, "Sometimes God calls you to seasons with people for a particular reason, so this might be a specific season God is calling you to." I remember thinking to myself, "Okay, sure, I get that. But this is more about me having a mentor for life in the place that I will call home forever. But thanks anyways."

Time went by and every single month I was challenged to dispute my "normal" and begin to notice the ways God was working, the things He was asking me to do, and the ways He was opening and closing doors every single day. As my mind began connecting the dots, I realized God was always chatting it up with me, it just did not look the way I thought it might. In one of our monthly meetings, I was anxiously attempting to piece together my this or my that, and Amy asked me the simplest, most profound question...

"What if instead of stressing about what God is asking you to do, *you just follow peace?*"

As we continued chatting, I realized that God is peace, therefore following peace is the equivalent of following God. In that split second, suddenly a thousand of my questions had answers; suddenly my anxious, swirling thoughts began to fall in an order that somehow seemed to make perfect sense; suddenly I knew the next steps I was supposed to take even if they truly seemed to make zero sense logically.

My husband and I were to open the door I was SURE would bring chaos – the dreaming door. One day as we were talking about how long we thought we'd stay in our current home before upgrading, God put a silly, crazy thought in our minds – what if it's not what home you will move to next, what if it's what city you will move to? Or even what state?

So, we began to dream and giggle at how absurd, random, and hilarious this conversation seemed to be. In that dreaming session, we dreamed up Greenville, South Carolina, which is somewhere that neither of us had ever even been. Both of us love to dream, laugh about it, and wake up the next day forgetting what we even talked about, but this time was different. We woke up the next day both very serious and quiet. One of us finally broke the silence and all we could muster was, "God isn't taking Greenville off my heart. I think we are supposed to seriously pray about moving there."

263

I now see how God had been putting our hearts in perfect unity from the beginning of the dreaming session where He laid Greenville on our hearts. So, as we began to pray, we began to research…then we planned a weekend trip to check it out…then we prayed some more…then we decided to put some feelers out for jobs…then prayed some more…then we both got job offers.

Throughout the entire process, I had the oddest sensation that I hadn't been very in tune with before then – peace.

Although we had specifically prayed for a perfect sign that listed the exact location, date, and time we were supposed to move (anyone else do this?), we did not get that. Instead, we got what God's Word promised us we'd get – His peace that surpasses all understanding that will continue to guard our hearts and minds in Jesus. We decided to follow that peace, because we were certain it also meant we were following God.

God is peace & peace is God.

Three months later, we moved to Greenville simply because God told us to. It's been terrifying, exhilarating, and invigorating. Since being here beautiful, peaceful chaos has ensued. God brought us here the exact week the church we felt called to be a part of began assembling their launch team for the new campus.

Who knows what this all means, but God is wrecking our plans day by day and there is truly nothing better than surrendering to it and getting to ride the waves instead of drowning in them.

~ Jess Ellis

...

Each of these stories captures a moment where God told one of His followers to do something and they said yes. With a heart of obedience, they set down their own desires and plans to pursue His.

Rather than living with their fists tightly closed, they lived with their hands wide open in surrender.

———

LIVING A LIFE OF SURRENDER IS THE
ONLY ONE WORTH LIVING.

———

It wasn't easy, pain free, or without frustration, but the fruit that came from their obedience was plentiful.

Living a life of surrender is the only one worth living.

You see, I don't want to look back on my life and see that my plans came to fruition.

Instead, I want my life to be made up of a million "because God told me to moments."

And that's the lasting thought I want to leave you with – what is your story going to be made up of?

Your plans, dreams, and desires?

Or a million "because God told me to moments?"

I WANT MY LIFE TO BE MADE UP OF A MILLION "BECAUSE GOD TOLD ME TO MOMENTS."

Take a Minute

Remember

- Our God cannot be simplified into words. He is far too great for that.
- It's easy to judge someone you don't know. It's much harder to judge someone who has shown you their heart.
- Our understanding of the Creator and Author of our lives grows each time we get a glimpse into a different story He has written.
- Each story is so different, but He is consistent.
- Living a life of surrender is the only one worth living.
- I want my life to be made up of a million "because God told me to moments."

Recite

"Jesus did many other things as well. If every one of them were written down, I suppose that even the whole world would not have room for the books that would be written."

John 21:25

Reflect

- Have you ever felt like you didn't have a testimony or one that wasn't worth sharing?
- Which one of the stories resonated with you most and why?
- What is something you learned about the character of God through the stories?

- Do you want your life to be made up of a million "because God told me to moments?" If so, what's your next step in making that happen?

Respond

Take a few minutes to talk with God about what is stirring in your heart. Ask Him to show you what your story is and who you can share it with. Do you want your life to be made up of a million "because God told me to moments?" Take a few minutes and think about your answer. If the answer is yes, ask God to show you what your next step might be to living a life of complete surrender.

One Last Thing

Whether or not I've met you, I want you to know I consider you a dear friend of mine. First, because if you actually read to the end of this book (or maybe you are the kind of reader who just skips to the end) you have just given me the sweetest gift. Second, you now know the depths of my heart and I only share that stuff with friends I love. And third, no matter how different our stories are, or our lives might be, I've got a feeling you and I have a lot in common and would have plenty to talk about.

I didn't really know what I was going to write about when God told me to write a book – but He carried me through.

I was terrified to give up my dream of teaching for a life that had less of a plan – but He is carrying me through.

It has hurt recognizing my dreams and plans needed to be let go of in order to embrace His – but He is carrying me through.

Some days I feel like I'm not even one step closer to sorting out my life. I'm simply living one day at a time.

Finding myself on my knees each morning while I rattle off my worries to Him and then send them floating down the river trusting He has it all figured out. Working to embrace each moment, opportunity, or obstacle that comes my way and knowing He makes no mistakes.

I don't know exactly where you are at right now or what you are going through, but I'm going to guess it's somewhere in the middle of trying to fully surrender to our Father while fighting the urge to grasp for control and answers.

As I've said before, welcome to the club.

You are not alone in this fight to daily die to self.

To choose Him and His will each day even when it's hard and it hurts.

It's a war I'll be waging until my last breath.

Before you close this book, there are a few things I want you to know.

You were created from the beginning with perfection in mind.

You are and always have been more loved than you could ever understand.

You have a calling on your life and our Father wants you to be a part of His Kingdom building.

When He calls you, He will equip you.

No matter what you have done, where you have come from, or where you are now, our God is in the business of redeeming and healing; nothing or no one is ever too far gone for Him.

No experience in your life is wasted. All things are redeemed and woven into a beautiful tapestry – a masterpiece – when you choose to surrender everything to Him.

He has a perfect story already written for you – just ask Him for the next step and He will show you the way.

He is the only way. So talk to Him, read His Word, and dive into a life lived alongside Him.

Pray big bold prayers and be ready for big, scary (but exciting) answers.

Lastly, there is unmatched power that comes from complete surrender.
Just let go and lay it at His feet. A life lived with hands open in
surrender is the only way to truly live.

I have been praying for you and will continue to pray for you. And hey, a friendship goes two ways, so because you just so graciously listened to my story, I'd love to hear yours. Do you have a "because God told me to moment" to share? I'm just a few finger-taps away…find me, friend me, and then introduce yourself. I'm always looking for new friends.

♡ Morgan

Now that you've read my story, and brief stories from several others, are you wondering what might be next for you?

My prayer is that maybe – just maybe – you're considering surrendering your life to God if you haven't already.

God wants nothing more than to be invited into your life as Father, friend, and leader. You don't have to be put together or healed or fixed to invite Him into your life, because He majors in taking your hurting, broken heart and making it beautiful.

God saw our sin and saw that we needed a Savior, so He sent His only son, Jesus, down to earth to die on a cross for our sins. For YOUR sins.

The only thing left for you to do is choose Him and then run to His arms to find healing, forgiveness, and unconditional love.

If this is a step you want to take, you can ask Him however you'd like, but if you want some guidance, here is a prayer to help give you the words.

Father, thank You for choosing me. Thank You for sending Your son to die on the cross for my sins. God, I ask that You come into my life. Forgive me of my sins. Be my leader and my friend. I want to follow You. I desire to know You. Today I surrender my life to You. Amen.

Friend, if you just prayed that prayer or something similar, please tell someone about it. This is the most important decision you will ever make, and it deserves to be celebrated. Heaven is rejoicing right now.

"In the same way, I tell you, there is rejoicing in the presence of the angels of God over one sinner who repents."

Luke 15:10

As for the next steps? I encourage you to find a local church to get involved in, start reading the Bible, listen to worship music, and seek out friends who will encourage you to grow nearer to Him.

And if you don't feel like you are ready to make this decision, that's okay. Keep praying, asking God to reveal Himself to you. He will show up. He always does.

To My Village...

To my heavenly Father, not a day goes by where I'm not incredibly grateful and humbled that You chose me – to be Your child and Your vessel. Thank you for entrusting me with Your message and for letting me be a part of Your Kingdom building. Help my eyes stay fixed on You.

To Jess, from our awkward first day as college roommates until now, you have spoken truth, wisdom, and encouragement into my life. Thank you for being my "Nathan" and having the boldness to say the hard things. You have cheered me on, every step of the way, and I am forever grateful.

To Kelsey, you've championed me since my middle school days and it's a gift I've never taken for granted. Your sweet and wise spirit is such a blessing to me. Thank you for always being one text or call away.

To the mentors and leaders who have taught me, shaped me, and prayed for me: Marilou McConaghie, Scotty Priest, Mark Groutas, Scott Lasher, Melissa Yocum, Cary Yocum, Jessa Johnson, and Russ Stutzman. Thank you for every ounce of time and energy you have poured into me. My faith is what it is because of you.

To my go-to girls who make my life richer, sweeter, and far more fun: McKenzie Brandt, Sam Bushlack, Ashtyn Dellamaestra, Briana Melkonian, Marie Bartlett, and Bri Young. I don't have to explain myself when I'm with you, you listen to me ramble, and you let me pick where to eat. Thank you for choosing to stick by my side.

To my editor, Royalene Doyle. You came into my life at the perfect moment, and I feel so grateful that these pages have been influenced by your wisdom. Thank you for letting His Spirit lead and for helping me get to the finish line.

Finally, to my people, the Colander crew: Mom, Dad, Michael, Mitchell, Maliyah, (and Coco). Because of you guys, I believe family is the greatest gift. It's where I find safety, security, consistency, laughter, and love. I couldn't do life without each of you. Thank you for everything.

And to everyone else in my village, you know who you are. I am blessed by you and I'm so thankful you are in my life.

To my new friend, I would love and appreciate your help!

Would you consider becoming a #BecauseGodToldMeTo ambassador?

Here's all it takes...

- Take a picture of yourself with the book, where you are reading it, or a page that inspired you, and share it on your social media platform.
- Write a book review on Goodreads, Amazon, or any other retailer site.
- Ask God who He wants you to share this book with and give them a copy as a gift.
- Recommend this book to your church, small group, workplace, or anywhere you are connected to.
- Follow me on social media and like, comment, and share any posts about this book.

I appreciate you more than you know.